CIPS STUDY MATTERS

CERTIFICATE IN
PROCUREMENT AND SUPPLY OPERATIONS

COURSE BOOK

Procurement and Supply Administration

© Profex Publishing Limited, 2016

Printed and distributed by:

The Chartered Institute of Procurement & Supply,
Easton House, Easton on the Hill, Stamford, Lincolnshire PE9 3NZ
Tel: +44 (0) 1780 756 777
Fax: +44 (0) 1780 751 610
Email: info@cips.org
Website: www.cips.org

First edition September 2012
Reprinted with minor amendments June 2016

Contents

Preface

Welcome to your new Course Book.

Your Course Book provides detailed coverage of all topics specified in the unit content.

For a full explanation of how to use your new Course Book, turn now to page ix. And good luck in your studies!

A note on style

Throughout your Course Books you will find that we use the masculine form of personal pronouns. This convention is adopted purely for the sake of stylistic convenience – we just don't like saying 'he/she' all the time. Please don't think this reflects any kind of bias or prejudice.

June 2016

The Unit Content

The unit content is reproduced below, together with reference to the chapter in this Course Book where each topic is covered.

Unit purpose and aim(s)

On completion of this unit, candidates will be able to explain how effective administration can ensure that timely deliveries are achieved by suppliers.

This unit will explain the necessary documentation and administrative processes that are involved in forming agreements with external suppliers.

Learning outcomes, assessment criteria and indicative content

Chapter

How to Use Your Course Book

Organising your study

'Organising' is the key word: unless you are a very exceptional student, you will find a haphazard approach is insufficient, particularly if you are having to combine study with the demands of a full-time job.

A good starting point is to timetable your studies, in broad terms, between now and the date of your assessment. How many subjects are you attempting? How many chapters are there in the Course Book for each subject? Now do the sums: how many days/weeks do you have for each chapter to be studied?

Remember:

- Not every week can be regarded as a study week – you may be going on holiday, for example, or there may be weeks when the demands of your job are particularly heavy. If these can be foreseen, you should allow for them in your timetabling.
- You also need a period leading up to the assessment in which you will revise and practise what you have learned.

Once you have done the calculations, make a week-by-week timetable for yourself for each paper, allowing for study and revision of the entire unit content between now and the date of your assessment.

Getting started

Aim to find a quiet and undisturbed location for your study, and plan as far as possible to use the same period each day. Getting into a routine helps avoid wasting time. Make sure you have all the materials you need before you begin – keep interruptions to a minimum.

Using the Course Book

You should refer to the Course Book to the extent that you need it.

- If you are a newcomer to the subject, you will probably need to read through the Course Book quite thoroughly. This will be the case for most students.
- If some areas are already familiar to you – either through earlier studies or through your practical work experience – you may choose to skip sections of the Course Book.

The content of the Course Book

This Course Book has been designed to give detailed coverage of every topic in the unit content. As you will see from pages vii–viii, each topic mentioned in the unit content is dealt with in a chapter of the Course Book. For the most part the order of the Course Book follows the order of the unit content closely, though departures from this principle have occasionally been made in the interest of a logical learning order.

Each chapter begins with a reference to the assessment criteria and indicative content to be covered in the chapter. Each chapter is divided into sections, listed in the introduction to the chapter, and for the most part being actual captions from the unit content.

All of this enables you to monitor your progress through the unit content very easily and provides reassurance that you are tackling every subject that is assessable.

Each chapter contains the following features.

- Clear coverage of each topic in a concise and approachable format
- A chapter summary
- Self-test questions

The study phase

For each chapter you should begin by glancing at the main headings (listed at the start of the chapter). Then read fairly rapidly through the body of the text to absorb the main points. If it's there in the text, you can be sure it's there for a reason, so try not to skip unless the topic is one you are familiar with already.

Then return to the beginning of the chapter to start a more careful reading. You may want to take brief notes as you go along.

Test your recall and understanding of the material by attempting the self-test questions. These are accompanied by cross-references to paragraphs where you can check your answers and refresh your memory.

The revision phase

Your approach to revision should be methodical and you should aim to tackle each main area of the unit content in turn. Re-read your notes. Then do some question practice. The CIPS website contains many past exam questions and you should aim to identify those that are suitable for the unit you are studying.

Additional reading

Your Course Book provides you with the key information needed for each module but CIPS strongly advocates reading as widely as possible to augment and reinforce your understanding. CIPS produces an official reading list of books, which can be downloaded from the bookshop area of the CIPS website.

To help you, we have identified one essential textbook for each subject. We recommend that you read this for additional information.

The essential textbook for this unit is *Purchasing and Supply Chain Management* by Kenneth Lysons and Brian Farrington.

Examination

This module is assessed by completion of 60 multiple choice questions in three hours. There will be 20 questions covering each of the three learning outcomes. You must get at least 15 out of the 20 right for each learning outcome in order to pass.

CHAPTER 1

Effective and Efficient Administration

Assessment criteria and indicative content

1.1 Define effective and efficient administration

- Defining administration
- Reviewing the steps taken to forming agreements made with suppliers
- Defining effectiveness and efficiency

1.2 Explain the administration of the pre contract stages of a sourcing process

- The creation of requisitions and requirements

Section headings

1 Administration, efficiency and effectiveness
2 Forming agreements with suppliers
3 The creation of requisitions and requirements

1 Administration, efficiency and effectiveness

Defining administration

1.1 There have been many attempts to define 'administration', and in particular to distinguish it from 'management'. For example, Laurie Mullins (in *Management and Organisational Behaviour*) writes: 'For our purposes administration is interpreted as part of the management process, and concerned with the design and implementation of systems and procedures to help meet stated objectives'.

1.2 Similarly, EFL Brech defined administration as 'that part of the management process concerned with the institution and carrying out of procedures by which the programme is laid down and communicated, and the progress of activities is regulated and checked against targets and plans'.

1.3 There seems to be consensus that administration is one part of a wider process described by the term 'management'.

Administration in procurement

1.4 Procurement administration is concerned with the operational relationship between the buyer and the supplier, the implementation of procedures defining the working methods and practices between them, and the smooth operation of routine administrative and clerical functions.

1.5 The importance of administration (both buyers' and suppliers' procedures) to the success of the purchase and to the relationship between them, should not be underestimated. Clear administrative procedures ensure that all parties understand who does what, when, and how.

1.6 Administration will require appropriate resourcing. It may be that the responsibility falls on a nominated individual. If not, and the responsibility is shared across a team, it is important that all members of the team deal promptly with administration tasks, particularly during the early stages of a purchase.

1.7 The procedures that usually make up administration are as follows.

- Procedure maintenance and change control
- Monitoring of charges and costs
- Ordering procedures
- Payment procedures
- Budget procedures
- Resource management and planning
- Management reporting
- Escalation
- Dispute resolution

1.8 These procedures should be designed to reflect the specific circumstances of the purchase and the organisation. Bear in mind that additional administrative procedures may also be needed.

1.9 Keeping a procedures manual up to date is an important activity, but it should not be a burden. The effort required may be reduced by ensuring that procedures are sufficiently flexible to enable *ad hoc* small-scale changes or adjustments within agreed parameters without needing to change the manual.

1.10 A system should be established to keep the manual up to date and to ensure that all documents relating to it are consistent, and that all parties have a common view. For a large or complex operation, a formal document management procedure is critically important. Some form of change control procedure is needed.

1.11 It is particularly important that exceptions should be carefully controlled. Formal authorisation procedures will be required to ensure that only those exceptions that can be justified in business terms are carried out.

1.12 Requirements for performance reports and management information should have been defined before and during contract negotiations, and confirmed during the transition period of the contract. It is likely that information requirements will change during the lifetime of the contract, which should be flexible enough to allow for this.

1.13 Where possible, use should be made of the supplier's own management information and performance measurement systems. Information may be required about all performance measures or only about exceptions – that is, instances when performance differs from what was expected. 'Exception reporting' minimises the time the buyer needs to assess performance and ensures attention is focused on areas that need it most.

Defining effectiveness and efficiency

1.14 Economy, efficiency and effectiveness – often abbreviated to 'the three Es' – are standard objectives pursued by departments and organisations in all sectors.

- Economy essentially means that we should not pay above the odds for an item or service, or any input that we purchase. If one supplier is offering Item X for $1.00 per unit, and another is charging $1.10 for the same item, then we should normally buy from the first supplier.
- Efficiency means that we should complete tasks without waste of inputs. If Product Y normally takes two units of Item X in its manufacture, and we manage to produce it using only 1.8 units, then we have been efficient. If it takes us 2.2 units of Item X, we have been inefficient.
- Effectiveness means that we accomplish tasks that fit in with overall objectives. It is not effective to manufacture units of Product Y if we are already overstocked with it, no matter how economically or efficiently we do it. Similarly, it is not effective if we have Product Y in stock but cannot convey it promptly to the internal or external customers who need it.

1.15 In a newly developed procurement function the initial emphasis may be on cost reduction, relating both to the cost of inputs and to the cost of running the procurement function. (The focus is on improving **efficiency**.) In a more developed procurement function, measures may be introduced for more strategic aspects of the role, such as supplier relationship management. (The focus is on improving **effectiveness**.)

1.16 Table 1.1 highlights some possible measures relating to both efficiency and effectiveness.

Table 1.1 *Efficiency and effectiveness of procurement*

MEASURES OF PROCUREMENT EFFICIENCY	MEASURES OF PROCUREMENT EFFECTIVENESS
Basic purchase price of inputs	Quality of output
Cost of placing an order	Quality of service to customers
Cost of staffing the procurement function	Achieving objectives within budget
Speed of transaction processing	Quality of supplier relationships
Use of information technology	Impact on profitability
Efficiency of organisational structure	Prompt delivery to customers
Efficiency of supplier management	

2 Forming agreements with suppliers

2.1 Contracts are a central feature of everyday life. The purchase of a study book, the boarding of a bus, the ordering of a meal in a restaurant: all constitute contracts. A contract is simply *an agreement between two (or more) parties which is intended to be legally binding*.

2.2 The 'legally binding' aspect makes a contract different from a social agreement, such as arranging to borrow a friend's car for the day. In the latter case, if one party does not carry out his part of the deal, he will not be taken to court by the other to enforce the agreement. If the agreement is between two commercial enterprises, however, it is presumed that there is an intention to 'enter into legal relations': that is, to use the law to enforce the agreement if necessary.

2.3 The law of contract is concerned with four basic questions.

- *Is there a contract in existence?* The fundamental requirement is that there must be a clear mutually understood 'agreement' between the parties, in the form of an offer and an acceptance.
- *Is the agreement one which the law should recognise and enforce?* Some contracts will be

wholly or partly invalid or unenforceable, because of undermining (or 'vitiating') factors such as a mistake or misunderstanding in what a party thought it was agreeing to.

- *When do the obligations of the parties come to an end?* The most common method of terminating a contract is when both parties have performed their agreed obligations to mutual satisfaction: the contract has been fulfilled. However, contracts can also be terminated by the failure of one or both parties to meet an essential term of the contract ('breach of contract').

- *What remedies are available for the injured party if the other party fails to meet its contractual obligations?* Possible remedies include the right to terminate all obligations under the contract (eg to refuse to pay for faulty goods) and monetary compensation for loss suffered as a result of the failure (damages).

2.4   In the 'offer and acceptance' at the heart of a contract:

- The 'offer' may be the seller's offer to sell (eg in the case of a tender bid or quotation, for example), which is accepted by the buyer to establish an agreement
- The 'offer' may be the buyer's offer to buy (eg in the case of an auction bid, for example), which the seller accepts in order to establish an agreement.

2.5   In either case, it should be clear that a key requirement for a valid and workable commercial agreement is the clear statement and accurate alignment of:

- Exactly **what the buyer wants** (in terms of goods and services – and how, when, at what cost and to what level of quality they will be supplied) *and*
- **What the supplier is offering**, or agrees to supply.

2.6   Defining and communicating the buyer's requirements, in such a way as to support a clear and unambiguous agreement, is therefore the basis for an effective commercial contract. Several different documents may be used for this purpose, and together they will make up the terms of understanding, or contract, between the two parties.

Defining and communicating the requirement

2.7   The buying organisation will seek to establish a detailed description of its requirements which can be communicated to potential suppliers. Detailed descriptions may already exist (if the purchase is a straight re-buy, for example), but for new or modified procurements, they may have to be drawn up, in the form of:

- Specifications (of various types)
- Service level agreements (added to the specification of services)
- Contract terms which set out the obligations of buyer and seller in relation to the fulfilment of the specification
- Key performance indicators, or performance measures which will be used to establish whether the requirement has been satisfactorily met.

2.8   A requirement can be signalled to prospective, pre-qualified or approved suppliers in various ways, depending on the sourcing policies of the organisation for particular types of purchase. For routine, low-value purchases or re-buys, for example, there may be framework agreements or call-off contracts in place. Or the buyer may simply be able to refer to approved suppliers' catalogues or price lists and make one-off purchases.

2.9   For more modified, new, non-standard or high-value requirements, the buyer may have to initiate negotiations with, or solicit proposals from, one or more suppliers, in order to develop an agreed understanding of what the buyer requires, and what the supplier is able to offer: in other words, the basis for a contract.

3 The creation of requisitions and requirements

3.1 Before any procurement transaction can even begin, someone must notice that something is needed which is not currently available. This need must be notified to the procurement department.

3.2 The need may be identified by a user department; for example, a designer may recognise a need for enhanced computer equipment or software for use in his work. Or the impetus may come from a stores department; perhaps the storekeeper's check on stock levels reveals a shortage of a component used in production.

3.3 In either of these cases the normal procedure would be for the department concerned to issue a purchase requisition. This form describes the item needed and instigates action by the procurement department. Typically, the originator of the requisition would keep a copy of the form while the other copy is forwarded as appropriate.

- If the originator is the stores department, the copy is forwarded to procurement for action.
- If the originator is a user department, the copy is forwarded to Stores. Stores will meet the need if the item is in stock, and if not will pass the copy on to Procurement.

3.4 The purchase requisition is the start of the formal procurement process, although it may be preceded by an informal enquiry. A need is identified by someone and the procurement department is notified. It may be necessary for Procurement to do some preliminary work before the user crystallises his requirements.

3.5 The purchase requisition form (whether printed or electronic) will be used by the procurement department to translate the user's requirement into a purchase order so it must contain sufficient information to allow them to do that. Of course, the amount of detail required may vary: a routine requirement for stock may require far less information than a one-off purchase of a major capital item.

3.6 A purchase requisition should include the following details.

- A *serial number*. This is a unique number which allows both the user and Procurement to easily identify each requisition.
- The *internal department code*, or budgetary code, to which the expenditure is to be charged
- The *name and signature* of the originator of the requisition, and its date. This may act as an official authorisation of the need, giving procurement authority to act upon it, so the signature should be that of an individual with appropriate authority.
- A *description of the product or service* required: identified by brand name or model number (if known), or accompanied by the specification (if already available)
- *Quantity*. Identifies how many the user needs.
- *Price*. Generally speaking the price of the product is not included on a requisition as it is the job of Procurement to buy the product at the most advantageous price. However, a maximum price or a target price might be specified.
- *Supplier*. Again, finding the best supplier is the job of Procurement but occasionally, a user may have a legitimate reason for buying from a particular supplier – perhaps to conduct a trial – so he might specify the supplier.

- *Delivery address*. Identifies the point to which the goods must be delivered. Normally this will be to a location within the organisation but it might be to a location outside the organisation such as a customer's warehouse. This will help to reduce the waste of time and effort caused by double handling the goods between the different locations.
- *Date required*. This usually specifies the latest date by which the goods must be delivered but it might specify the only day on which the goods must be delivered.

3.7 In some cases the identification of need is signalled not on a purchase requisition, but on a **bill of materials**, essentially the 'shopping list' compiled by a resource requirements planning system.

3.8 Requisition and bill of materials forms will contain details of the required item(s) in a standardised form. However, Procurement will not simply act on this description without enquiry. It may be appropriate to refer the requisition back to the originator: for clarification, or to challenge over-specification or unnecessary variation, to reduce unnecessary purchases, or to suggest alternatives that will offer better quality or lower price than the item requisitioned.

3.9 Challenging purchase requisitions and specifications may add value both economically and environmentally.

3.10 Procurement should not make changes without consultation because they cannot know all the factors that the originator may have had in mind when drawing up the requisition. But neither should they accept requisitions without question.

Chapter summary

- Administration is 'part of the management process ... concerned with the design and implementation of systems and procedures to help meet stated objectives'.
- Economy means we pay $1.00 per unit rather than $1.10. Efficiency means that we complete tasks without waste of inputs. Effectiveness means that we accomplish tasks that fit with overall objectives.
- A contract is a legally enforceable agreement by which each of two parties binds himself to provide some kind of benefit to the other party.
- A buyer will often ask a supplier to make an offer of supplying goods or services, perhaps by a request for quotation or an invitation to tender. If the offer is acceptable, the buyer may contract on that basis and a supply contract comes into being.
- It is common for the buyer to communicate his requirements by means of a specification.
- The need for something to be bought is communicated to the procurement department by means of a purchase requisition.

Self-test questions

Numbers in brackets refer to the paragraphs where you can check your answers.

1   List typical procedures involved in administration. (1.7)

2   Distinguish between economy, efficiency and effectiveness. (1.14)

3   What are the four basic questions at the heart of contract law? (2.3)

4   What documents may be used to define the buyer's requirements? (2.7)

5   List details that will typically appear on a purchase requisition. (3.6)

6   What is a bill of materials? (3.7)

CHAPTER 2

Pre-Contract Administration

Assessment criteria and indicative content

 Explain the administration of the pre contract stages of a sourcing process

- The use of specifications, key performance indicators (KPIs), and contract terms
- The creation of requests for quotations or invitations to tender
- The use of pre-qualification questionnaires
- The submission of quotations or tenders for requirements
- The assessment of quotations and tenders

Section headings

1 Quotation and tender documents
2 Specifications
3 Key performance indicators
4 Contract terms and schedules
5 Pre-qualification questionnaires

1 Quotation and tender documents

Request for quotation

1.1 One approach to initiating dealings with a supplier is to send an enquiry, 'request for information', 'request for quotation' (RFQ) or 'request for proposal' (RFP) to one or more suppliers. Suppliers may sometimes send in proposals without being asked, for standard items, or if the buyer's requirements are known (eg from market exchanges or directories).

1.2 Whether or not a formal tendering procedure is being used, it is common for a buyer to contact a number of suppliers in search of quotations. Often the buyer's enquiry will be communicated using a pre-printed form. This makes life simpler for the buyer, ensures that important points of concern are not overlooked, and makes it easier to compare quotations from suppliers when they are eventually received.

1.3 A standard enquiry or RFQ form will typically set out the details of the requirement.

- The contact details of the purchaser
- A reference number to use in reply, and the date by which to reply
- The quantity and description of goods or services required
- The required place and date of delivery
- The buyer's standard terms and conditions of purchase, as well as any special terms
- Terms of payment

1.4   It will then invite the supplier(s) to submit a proposal and price (a 'quotation') for the contract. Quotations may be evaluated in various ways.

- On a comparative or 'competitive bidding' basis: eg the best value bid or quotation 'wins' the contract (as in competitive bidding or tendering)
- As a basis for negotiation with a preferred supplier (eg if a preferred or approved supplier is asked to present a quotation as the basis for negotiation to refine contract terms)
- As a way of 'testing the market': checking the current market price for requirements coming up for contract renewal.

1.5   It is worth noting that there are ethical issues in the use of requests for quotation, which may be the subject of procurement ethical codes. It is not ethical practice to seek quotations if there is no intention to purchase; or to seek quotations from multiple suppliers if you have already decided where the contract will be awarded. This is sometimes done to check the competitiveness of a current supplier, to 'motivate' a preferred supplier or to provide leverage in negotiation with a preferred supplier. But such practices are nowadays regarded as unethical. Potential suppliers are being misled by a false hope of work, and the preparation of quotations costs them time and resources.

1.6   Where the request for information is being used in anticipation of price negotiations with one or more suppliers, the buyer may also request appropriate cost data in support of the price proposal. If the buyer requires right of access to the supplier's cost records, this must also be established during the enquiry phase of the procurement, when potential suppliers believe that there is active competition for the job.

1.7   Suppliers will usually respond to the enquiry by supplying a quotation, representing their best price for supplying the buyer's stated requirements. If sufficiently comprehensive and detailed (capable of acceptance without further qualification), it may be regarded, in terms of the formation of a valid contract, as constituting an 'offer' which the buyer may or may not wish to accept.

Invitation to tender

1.8   The organisation may prefer to use a more formalised *competitive bidding* or tendering procedure, in which pre-qualified suppliers are issued with an invitation to tender (ITT), or an invitation to bid for a contract, with the buyer intending to choose the supplier submitting the best proposal or the lowest price.

1.9   Lysons & Farrington define tendering as 'a purchasing procedure whereby potential suppliers are invited to make a firm and unequivocal offer of the price and terms on which they will supply specified goods or services which, on acceptance, shall be the basis of the subsequent contract'.

1.10   A full competitive bidding or tendering process may typically be required for contracts over a certain value threshold, in order to ensure the competitiveness of supply.

1.11   Tendering, at its simplest, is the process by which suppliers are invited to put themselves forward (or 'bid') for a contract. There are several approaches to this.

- **Open tendering**, in which the invitation to tender is widely advertised and open to any potential bidder.
- **Selective tendering**, in which potential suppliers are pre-qualified (eg on the basis of their

technical competence and financial standing) and 3–10 suppliers are shortlisted for invitation to tender.

- **Restricted open tenders**, in which prospective suppliers are invited to compete for a contract, but are partly pre-qualified by advertising of the tender being restricted (eg to appropriate technical journals)

1.12   A best-practice tender procedure would include the following steps for the **preparation of the invitation to tender**.

- Preparation of detailed specifications and draft contract documents, setting out the requirement in detail: this is important in providing tender information to potential bidders, so that bids can be (a) accurately costed and (b) directly compared. Once the tender procedure is in motion, there is little room for re-negotiation and adjustment of specifications. Attention must be given to accurate specification of the requirement, including non-price criteria (eg quality measures or sustainability standards), so that the buyer's task will later be simply to (a) check that tenders received comply with the requirements, and (b) choose the lowest price (or best value) bid.
- Advertisement of the requirement, tender procedures to be followed, and timetables for expression of interest (in a selective tender) or submission of bids (in an open tender)
- Sending out of pre-qualification questionnaires (in a selective tender) in response to expressions of interest, with timescales for these to be returned. Follow-up information or clarification may be sought as part of the pre-qualification or appraisal process.
- Issue of invitation to tender (ITT) and tender documentation to those responding to the advertisement or invitation to tender within the prescribed time frame. Tender documents would normally include: an invitation to tender (ITT) and instructions to tenderers; a pricing document and/or form of tender; the specification; criteria for contract award; contract conditions or conditions of purchase; deadlines for submission; and a pre-addressed tender return label.
- Tender documents should be issued to each potential supplier in identical terms and by the same date.
- Tenders or offers will be received (in the form of sealed bids) for opening by the tender evaluation team, following the closing date for submission. The details of all tenders received will be logged, with the main details of each listed on an analysis sheet or spreadsheet for ease of comparison. Each tender will then be analysed, according to the specified criteria for contract award, with a view to selecting the 'best offer'.
- Post-tender clarification, verification of supplier information, and/or negotiation, where required.
- The contract will be awarded, and the award notified to tenderers. A best practice tender will also include 'de-briefing': the giving of feedback, on request, to unsuccessful tenderers, to enable them to improve the competitiveness of future bids, to develop the market – and to help the procurement function to improve future tender processes.

Assessment of quotations and tenders

1.13   The general principle is that the successful tender will be the one with the lowest price or the 'most economically advantageous tender' or MEAT (defined on the basis of whatever value criteria have been specified). However:

- The evaluation team may need to analyse whether and how effectively each bid meets the requirements of the specification, especially if performance, outcome or 'functional' specifications are used. Such specifications define the requirement in terms of performance, functionality or outcomes – without prescribing how these will be achieved. They are specifically designed to allow maximum flexibility for suppliers in coming up with value-adding, innovative solutions to the requirement.

- There may be considerable variety in the total solution 'package' being offered by bids: one may be more attractive than another (innovative, environmentally friendly, risk-reducing, value-adding) – even if price tells against it. Non-price criteria will have to be reviewed with particular care (and more details sought, if required), especially if suppliers have not been pre-qualified on these criteria.

1.14 It will be important, therefore, for any invitation to tender to state clearly that:

- The buyer will *not* be bound to accept the lowest price quoted (especially in the case of open tenders, where there has been no pre-qualification of suppliers)
- Specified non-price criteria (such as environmental or social sustainability or innovation) will be taken into account, and given a specified weighting or priority in the contract award decision.
- Post-tender negotiation may be entered into, if necessary to qualify or clarify tenders, or to discuss potential improvements or adjustments to suppliers' offers. In general, any fine-tuning or clarification of the winning tender should not alter the basics of the offer – as this would inject a new element, on which other bidders did not have an opportunity to compete.

1.15 The following guidelines summarise the main points to take account of in analysing tenders: Table 2.1.

Table 2.1 *A checklist for analysing tenders*

1.	Establish a routine for receiving and opening tenders, distributing copies as appropriate and ensuring security.
2.	Set out clearly the responsibilities of the departments involved.
3.	Establish objective award criteria. These should have been set out in the initial invitation to tender, particularly if the contract is subject to statutory control.
4.	Establish teams for the appraisal of each tender, ensuring that the required team members will be available during the time they are required.
5.	Establish a standardised format for logging and reporting on tenders.
6.	Check that the tenders received comply with the award criteria. Non-price criteria (eg technical and production capability, financial stability, environmental policies, or quality assurance accreditation) will need to be carefully reviewed (and more details sought if required), if suppliers have not been pre-qualified.
7.	Check the arithmetical accuracy of each tender!
8.	Eliminate suppliers whose total quoted price is above the lowest quotes by a specified percentage. (For example, eliminate any supplier whose quoted price is more than 20% above the average of the lowest two quotes.)
9.	Evaluate the tenders in accordance with predetermined checklists for technical, contractual and financial details.
10.	Prepare a report on each tender for submission to the project manager (and as a basis for feedback to unsuccessful bidders, where relevant).

2   Specifications

2.1   A specification can be simply defined as a statement of the requirements to be satisfied in the supply of a product or service.

2.2   The purpose of an effective specification is to:

- *Define the requirement* – encouraging all relevant stakeholders (including the procurers and users of the supplied items) to consider what they really need, and whether this is the only, most cost-effective or most value-adding solution
- *Communicate the requirement* clearly to suppliers, so that they can plan to conform – and perhaps also use their expertise to come up with innovative or lower-cost solutions to the requirement
- *Minimise risk and cost* associated with doubt, ambiguity, misunderstanding or dispute as to requirement, and what constitutes satisfactory quality and fitness for purpose
- *Provide a means of evaluating the quality or conformance* of the goods or services supplied, for acceptance (if conforming to specification) or rejection (if non-conforming), to ensure that 'right quality' is achieved, and to minimise failure costs
- *Support standardisation and consistency,* where items are procured from more than one source.

2.3   There are two main types of specification: conformance specification and performance (or functional) specification.

2.4   With a **conformance specification**, the buyer details exactly what the required product, part or material must *consist of*. The supplier may not know in detail, or even at all, what function the product will play in the buyer's business. The task is simply to *conform to the description* provided by the buyer.

2.5   A conformance specification may take any of the following forms.

- An *engineering drawing, design or blueprint* (technical or design specification): commonly used in engineering and construction or architecture environments, which require a high degree of technical accuracy and very tight tolerances (because of the complexity of assembly and machine function)
- A *chemical formula or 'recipe' of ingredients or materials* (composition specification): commonly used where particular physical properties (eg strength, flexibility or durability) are important for safety or performance (eg the metal used in car manufacture) or where materials are restricted by law, regulation or codes of practice, for health, safety or environmental reasons (eg the use of lead in paint)
- The specification of a *brand name and model name or number,* if a marketed product meets the buyer's criteria. Branded products tend to be of good quality and easy to source, if available. Procurement by brand may be essential if a particular part or material is patented or prestigious.
- A *sample* of the product, with a requirement for the supplier simply to duplicate the features and performance of the sample. This is a quick and easy method of specifying requirement without having to describe it, and offers some assurance (eg the ability to test the sample for suitability, prior to procurement)
- The specification of *compliance with a recognised standard* (eg British Standards, market grades, or International Standards): offering certified quality assurance and uniformity (standardisation).

2.6 A **performance (or functional) specification** is a relatively brief document (compared to a conformance specification), in which the buyer describes what he expects a part or material to be able to *achieve*, in terms of the functions it will perform, the level of performance it should reach, or the desired outcomes or outputs of its operation – within the constraints of any relevant input parameters and operating conditions. It is up to the supplier to furnish a product with will *satisfy these requirements*. The specification defines the functionality or performance to be achieved – but (unlike a conformance specification) does *not* prescribe *how* they are to be achieved (in terms of materials, designs or processes).

2.7 A typical performance specification might include the following details.

- The functionality, performance or capabilities to be achieved, within specified tolerances (or the outcomes of a process, or the outputs of a system)
- Key process inputs which will contribute to performance, including available utilities, user capability and training, and so on
- The operating environment and conditions in which the performance is to be achieved (and any extreme or unusual conditions in which it is not expected)
- How the product is required to interface with other elements of the process
- Required quality levels (including relevant standards)
- Required safety levels and controls (including relevant standards)
- Required environmental performance levels and controls (including relevant standards)
- Criteria and methods to be used to measure whether the desired function, performance or outcomes have been achieved.

2.8 To summarise therefore, the role of a specification is to define and communicate the buyer's requirements, in terms of either:

- *Conformance:* the buyer details exactly what the required product, part or material must consist of, and a product of 'satisfactory quality' is one which conforms to the description provided by the buyer – or
- *Performance:* the buyer describes what he expects the supplied item to be able to achieve. A product which is 'fit for purpose' is one which will satisfy these requirements: the buyer specifies the 'ends' (purposes) to be satisfied, and the supplier has relative flexibility about the 'means' of achieving them. This approach offers potential for innovative, collaborative, value-adding solutions. It also widens the potential supply market to include smaller, more innovative suppliers (who might be prevented from competing by prescriptive solutions or standards).

2.9 Compared with conformance specifications, performance specifications have a number of advantages, which have made them increasingly popular.

- Performance specifications are easier and cheaper to draft, compared to a more detailed, prescriptive (conformance) approach.
- The efficacy of the specification does not depend on the technical knowledge of the buyer (unlike conformance specifications). Suppliers may well know better than the buyer what is required, and how it can best be manufactured.
- Suppliers can use their full expertise, technologies and innovative capacity to develop optimum, lowest-cost solutions (where conformance specifications are prescriptive and inflexible).
- A greater share of specification risk is borne by the supplier: if the part supplied does not perform its function, the buyer is entitled to redress (whereas, with a conformance specification, the specifier bears responsibility for the functionality of the finished result).

- The potential supply base is wider than with a conformance specification. If the task is to supply something – anything – that will perform a particular function, the expertise of different suppliers could potentially provide a wide range of solutions.

2.10   It is particularly appropriate to use performance specifications in the following circumstances.

- Suppliers have greater relevant technical and manufacturing expertise than the buyer – so that the best knowledge is being used and leveraged. It should also be noted that the buyer will be highly reliant on the supplier's expertise: this puts pressure on effective supplier selection and evaluation.
- Technology is changing rapidly in the supplying industry – so that the buyer is not in a position of specifying yesterday's methodologies, but gets the best out of suppliers' innovation capacity and technological development.
- There are clear criteria for evaluating alternative solutions put forward by suppliers competing for the contract. These should be clearly communicated to potential suppliers, who may invest considerable time and resources in coming up with proposals, and will want to be assured that the selection process is fair.
- The buyer has sufficient time and expertise to assess the potential functionality of suppliers' proposals and competing alternatives (particularly if the supplier is using technology with which the buyer is unfamiliar). The complexity of the evaluation process is the major disadvantage of the performance specification approach.

2.11   The use of specification as a basis for a commercial agreement raises several issues for buyers.

- Specifications must clearly, comprehensively and unambiguously set out exactly what the buyer's (and other key stakeholders') expectations and requirements are. Otherwise, a supplier or bid may conform to specification and *still* not represent 'right quality'.
- Specification may be the best and last opportunity for buyers to build in qualitative, values-based criteria such as social or environmental sustainability or compatibility, which would otherwise be seen as too subjective to be used either in the directly competitive stage of contract award or in post-award contract management.

Specifying services

2.12   Services (and service elements) present buyers with problems additional to those that arise in purchasing materials or manufactured goods, when it comes to specifying requirements.

- Services are intangible and lack 'inspectability': specifying service levels – and subsequently checking whether or how far they have been achieved – is therefore very difficult. As Steve Kirby notes: 'How clean is clean? How long should it take to repair a computer? What is the definition of a well-cooked meal?'
- Services are variable: every separate instance of service provision is unique, because the personnel and circumstances are different. It is hard to standardise requirements.
- Services are provided in 'real time': transport, accommodation and catering services, for example, are only relevant when they are needed. Specifications therefore need to include the time of provision, so that the supplier can schedule provision accordingly.
- Many services can only be performed in particular locations (eg accommodation provided at a hotel premises, cleaning provided at the buyer's offices). Specifications may need to include explicit understandings about where the service is to be provided, the access required and related issues (such as confidentiality, if suppliers are working on the buyers' premises).
- A service may be procured for a long contract period, during which requirements may change from the original specification, requiring review, flexibility and change controls.

2.13 The more work that can be done at the pre-contract stage, the better. This means negotiating and agreeing service levels, schedules and the basis for charges in as much detail as possible before the legal contract is signed: disputes often stem from differing expectations on the part of buyer and supplier.

3 Key performance indicators

Performance measures and targets

3.1 Supplier performance measurement is the assessment and comparison of a supplier's current performance against:

- *Defined performance criteria* (such as quality standards and specific key performance indicators set out in a contract, service level agreement or continuous improvement agreement), to establish whether the aimed-for or agreed level of performance has been achieved
- *Previous performance,* to identify deterioration or improvement trends
- *The performance of other comparable organisations* (eg other suppliers) or standard *benchmarks*, to identify areas where performance falls short of best practice or the practice of competitors, and where there is therefore room for improvement.

3.2 Performance measurement is important because it supports the planning and control of operations and relationships: it is often said that 'what gets measured, gets managed'. It is intended to lead to performance improvement and supplier development, by identifying areas in which suppliers' current performance falls short of desired, competitive or best-practice levels. It is an important tool for communicating with stakeholders about their part in supply chain performance, and how they are doing. Performance measures, such as KPIs, can be used to manage, motivate and reward individuals, teams and suppliers.

3.3 Performance measures, or key performance indicators, incorporated in contracts with external suppliers, also define the buying organisation's expectations in regard to performance. In other words, they define the business need in terms of measurable outputs, outcomes or behaviours which 'indicate' that the required level of performance to meet the need has been met.

3.4 Supplier performance appraisal can then be used – both for individual contracts (as part of contract management) and for the aggregate performance of multiple contracts over time (vendor rating) for the following purposes.

- To help identify the highest-quality and best-performing suppliers: assisting decision-making regarding: (a) which suppliers should get specific orders; (b) when a supplier should be retained or removed from a preferred or approved list; (c) which suppliers show potential for more strategic partnership relationships; and (d) how to distribute the spend for an item among several suppliers, to manage risk
- To suggest how relationships with suppliers can be (or need to be) enhanced to improve their performance (eg to evaluate the effectiveness of Procurement's supplier selection and contract management processes)
- To help ensure that suppliers live up to what was promised in their contracts
- To provide suppliers with an incentive to maintain and/or continuously improve performance levels
- To significantly improve supplier performance, by identifying problems that can be tracked and fixed, or areas in which support and development is needed

3.5   Our focus here is on preparing the crucial groundwork for contract and performance management, by setting up the 'yardsticks' or measures by which contract compliance and conformance will be evaluated.

Key performance indicators

3.6   KPIs are clear qualitative or quantitative statements which define adequate or desired performance in key areas (or critical success factors), and against which progress and performance can be measured.

3.7   The key point about KPIs is that they state performance goals or expectations in a way that is capable of direct, detailed, consistent measurement at operational level, using available data collection systems.

3.8   Some of the benefits of using KPIs as performance measures are as follows.

- Increased and improved (results-focused) communication on performance issues
- Motivation to achieve or surpass the specified performance level (particularly with KPI-linked incentives, rewards or penalties). Motivation is in any case stronger where there are clear targets to aim for.
- Support for collaborative buyer-supplier relations, by enabling integrated or two-way performance measurement (with KPIs on both sides of the relationship)
- The ability directly to compare year on year performance, to identify improvement or deterioration trends
- Focus on key results areas (critical success factors) such as cost reduction and quality improvement
- Clearly defined shared goals, facilitating cross-functional and cross-organisational teamwork and relationships
- Reduced conflict arising from causes such as goal confusion and unclear expectations.

3.9   Setting KPIs for *supplier* performance, in particular, may be beneficial in the following areas.

- Setting clear performance criteria and expectations: motivating compliance and improvement
- Managing supply risk: controlling quality, delivery, value for money and so on
- Supporting contract management (to ensure that agreed benefits are obtained)
- Providing feedback for learning and continuous improvement in the buyer-supplier relationship – both for the supplier, and for the procurement department.

3.10   It is worth noting that KPIs can have some disadvantages as well. The pursuit of individual KPIs can lead to some dysfunctional or sub-optimal behaviour: cutting corners on quality or service to achieve productivity or time targets, say, or units focusing on their own targets at the expense of cross-functional collaboration and co-ordination. Targets will have to be carefully set with these potential problems in mind.

3.11   Standard KPIs or performance measures may be used by an organisation for certain types of routine contracts and common procurements. KPIs will not have to be systematically developed, using rigorous analysis, in all circumstances – and indeed, such a process would not be justified on cost-benefit grounds for low-value, routine purchases. However, for complex, high-value, new-buy contracts and projects, it may be necessary and justifiable to apply a systematic process to develop suitable performance measures.

3.12   You don't want to specify too many KPIs for a given contract: only those that are indicative measures of performance in areas necessary to achieve critical success factors. Otherwise, it will be too complicated and costly to monitor and measure performance – and the supplier may find the pursuit of multiple KPIs too complex. Eight to ten well-formulated KPIs may be realistic for any given planning and control period.

3.13 Effective communication is essential in KPI development. The buyer will need to be able to explain to the supplier exactly what performance standard is expected. The buyer may issue recent history trend data (if available), with a written explanation of key issues and requirements. For complex high-value new-buy contracts, for which the effort is justified, buyers should involve suppliers in the joint development of KPIs – rather than simply negotiating their agreement with KPIs already formulated. Suppliers may be able to contribute valuable expertise and experience to the process, and consultation creates a better likelihood of 'buy in' or commitment to jointly-developed KPIs.

Sample KPIs

3.14 There are a number of critical success factors in a supplier's performance that a buyer may want to evaluate, and a range of key performance indicators can be selected for each. In an exam, as in professional practice, you will obviously need to select or devise those most relevant to the context and (if specified by the question) the type of contract. For a general supply contract, however, performance measures may be applied to factors such as costs and cost management; quality; delivery performance; and service performance.

3.15 Each of these can be defined using a number of possible measures.

- A specific agreed standard or KPI, set out in the supply contract
- An established industry norm, standard or benchmark
- Past performance (eg using a year-on-year improvement percentage)
- The benchmark performance of other suppliers, including former suppliers of the same product or service (eg in measuring an outsourced service provider against the previous in-house provision of the service).

3.16 Some typical KPIs which might be incorporated in a contractual agreement (for a generic standard supply contract) are listed in Table 2.2.

Table 2.2 *General KPIs for supplier performance*

SUCCESS FACTORS	SAMPLE KPIs
Cost management	• Value or percentage of cost reductions obtained • Number of cost reduction initiatives proposed or implemented • Percentage range of acceptable cost variance from budgeted costs
Quality performance, conformance or compliance	• Percentage or volume of rejects and returns, errors or scrapped items delivered • Number of customer complaints (eg from users or end customers) and/or returns • Certification under quality management standards (eg ISO 9000) and/or environmental management standards (eg ISO 14001)
Timeliness and delivery	• Frequency or percentage of late, incorrect or incomplete deliveries • Percentage of on time in full – OTIF – deliveries • Range of acceptable schedule variance (deadline +/– x hours or days)
Service	• Promptness in dealing with enquiries and problems
Resources	• Minimum number of staff or resources of specified grades to be allocated to the project

3.17 KPIs may be expressed as simple, observable or measurable statements, defining acceptable performance. A basic example, again for a generic contract, might be as follows: Table 2.3.

Table 2.3 *KPIs as statements of performance*

PERFORMANCE CRITERION	PERFORMANCE INDICATOR
Quality	Management systems and processes are clear and documented
Cost management	Consumable procurement rates are benchmarked for value for money
Timeliness	Service is delivered within the agreed periods of availability
Quantity	Stocks are maintained to appropriate levels to ensure continuity of service
Compliance	Corporate policies and procedures are adhered to

4 Contract terms and schedules

4.1 The role of a contract is to set out the agreed roles, rights and obligations of both parties in a commercial transaction or relationship. A contract implies an intention to 'enter into legal relations': that is, both parties agree to be legally bound by the specified roles and responsibilities. It may take the form of a verbal agreement or 'understanding' (eg based on a regular trading relationship that has developed over time), but more complex contracts are usually formalised in writing.

Contract terms

4.2 Contract terms are statements by the parties to the contract as to what they understand their rights and obligations to be under the contract. They define the content of the 'offer' (or counter-offer) which becomes binding once accepted by the other party.

4.3 Contract terms define both parties' rights and obligations, and it is important that there should be genuine and specific agreement on what these are, from the outset. After the contract has been made, it is too late for either party to alter its terms unilaterally: such a variation is effective only if it is made by mutual agreement (ie by another contract).

4.4 Terms can be expressly or explicitly inserted into a contract by either or both of the parties (*express terms*) or can be implied or assumed to be included in the contract (*implied terms*) because they are a recognised part of the law.

- **Express terms** are clearly stated and recognised in the contract between the parties. The most common examples of express terms would be where the parties specify price, delivery dates, how carriage and insurance costs will be shared, and so on. Another example is an exclusion or exemption clause, which states that one party will not be liable (or will have only limited liability) for some specific breach of contract, or a *force majeure* clause which specifies special circumstances in which a party will not be liable for failure to fulfil its contract obligations.
- **Implied terms** are terms which are assumed to exist by virtue of accepted legal principles, such as *caveat emptor* or 'buyer beware', and statute (legislation). They therefore form part of the contract – whether or not they are mentioned within it. For example it is common for statute to imply certain terms into all contracts for the sale of goods – such as the buyer's right to expect goods supplied to be of satisfactory quality and fit for purpose. The printed terms and conditions of a contract cannot be viewed in isolation: buyers and suppliers must

bear in mind that they may have responsibilities or rights not specifically dealt with in the terms of the contract.

4.5 Usually, each term of a contract can be classified as either a 'condition' or a 'warranty'.

- A **condition** is a vital term of the contract, breach of which may be treated by the innocent party as a substantial failure to perform a basic element of the agreement. In such a case, the innocent party has the option of treating the contract as ended (releasing it from any further obligations) and claiming damages for any loss suffered.
- A **warranty** is a less important term which is incidental to the main purpose of the contract. Breach of a warranty does not constitute a substantial failure of performance, so the whole agreement need not collapse. The innocent party may claim damages for the breach, but cannot 'repudiate' (reject) the contract.

4.6 The contract may expressly declare that some term is to be a condition. One important example is when the *time of performance* is declared to be 'of the essence of the contract' (so that late delivery would be considered a breach of condition, rather than a breach of warranty).

Standard contracts and model form contracts

4.7 Most commercial concerns do not go to the trouble of drawing up a special contract every time they procure or sell goods or services. For most routine transactions, they rely on standard terms. Each firm will draw up its own 'standard terms of business', and will seek to ensure that these terms are accepted by other firms with whom they deal. It is common for organisations to publish their standard terms wherever possible: on purchase order forms, order acknowledgements, invoices, receipts and so on.

4.8 For more complex and/or larger, more strategically critical, high-risk or non-routine purchases, standard terms are very unlikely to include the level of detail, and specific provisions, that need to be addressed in the contract. In such cases, it would be worth the time and expense of negotiation and drafting of contract-specific terms and conditions.

4.9 Another advantage of negotiating contracts with suppliers, agreeing specific terms and conditions – which may include some of the buyer's standard terms and some of the seller's – is that it avoids any ambiguity or conflict about whose terms apply in a given situation.

4.10 However, it would be extremely time-consuming and expensive to negotiate and formulate contract terms and clauses afresh for every new contract. In many situations, it would also be a case of 'reinventing the wheel', since the terms would be substantially similar for most business dealings of a similar type.

4.11 Where an organisation has recurring dealings with a supplier, or recurring requirements for a product or service, it may develop its own **standard contract** for use in particular types of dealings. For example, a publisher might have a standard contract for authors, another for printers, another covering sale to book distributors and another for sale to bookshops. Each standard contract would incorporate standard terms and conditions which have proved acceptable and workable in each type of contractual relationship in the past. A supplier or buyer could accept the contract as it stands, or negotiate to vary specific terms.

4.12 **Model form contracts** are published by third party experts (such as trade associations and professional bodies), incorporating standard practice in contracting for specific purposes within specific industries, and ensuring a fair balance of contractual rights and responsibilities for buyer and seller. For example, CIPS publishes a range of model form contracts and contract clauses, which members are licensed to use in support of their employment. A number of professional bodies in the fields of engineering and construction have also developed comprehensive model form contracts for design, engineering and construction projects.

4.13   The *advantages and disadvantages* of using standard and model form contracts are summarised in Table 2.4

Table 2.4 *Advantages and disadvantages of standard and model form contracts*

ADVANTAGES	DISADVANTAGES
Helps reduce time and costs of contract development (including legal costs)	Terms may not be as advantageous to a powerful buyer as if contract was negotiated
Avoids 'reinventing the wheel' – but can be adapted to suit particular circumstances	Terms may not include special clauses or requirements to cover the buyer's position
Industry model forms are widely accepted, reducing negotiation time and costs	Legal advice is still required if significant amendments or variations are to be made
Designed to be fair to both parties	Costs of training buyers to use model forms

Contract schedules

4.14   In legal contracts, the term 'addendum' (or 'appendix' or 'annexe') is used for an additional document, not included in the main part of the contract but referred to within it, which may contain additional terms, specifications, provisions, standard forms or other information. Addenda are often used in standard form contracts – in the same way that appendices are used in formal reports – to make changes or add more specific details, cross-referenced to the specific clause in the contract which is being modified or clarified.

4.15   There are two main types of addendum to a contract.

- Contract **schedules**, usually providing additional or more detailed and numerical information (such as pricing schedules and non-disclosure agreements), which can be separately referred to for detail on particular supplementary areas.
- Contract **exhibits**, containing examples of any standard forms, evidences or models referred to in the contract.

Pricing schedules

4.16   The main contract may contain a fairly simple pricing clause, such as the following.

'The price of the goods and/or services shall be as stated in the appended pricing agreement [Schedule A]. No increase will be accepted by the buyer unless agreed by him in writing in advance of delivery or performance.'

4.17   The pricing schedule may then include details of the standard or negotiated agreement on:

- The terms of the pricing agreement applied to the contract: for example, a fixed price agreement or a cost-plus agreement (where the buyer agrees to pay a price that covers all the supplier's costs and also a profit margin for the supplier)
- The supplier's schedule of prices, fees and charges, or agreed fees and charges

- The pricing mechanism to be used in calculating the price, if the price is to be determined by the supplier's costs (list of allowable costs, target costs or range of costs), labour hours spent (rate per hour for different grades of staff) and so on
- Formulae or indices to be used in assessing supplier claims for price adjustment (contract price adjustment clauses)
- Incentive payments or gain-sharing formulae to be used to reward the supplier for attainment of cost savings or other specified KPIs
- Discounts available to the buyer (percentages and qualification criteria, such as volume purchase, prompt payment)
- Price-related penalties for non-performance (eg late payment penalties)
- Agreements on pricing instalments or stage payments (where relevant).

Schedule of contract documents

4.18 A schedule may be compiled to specify the documents which comprise the contract. For example, the schedule of contract documents may state that: 'The services and goods shall be provided in accordance with the following documents, which comprise the contract:

1 Letter of acceptance of tender
2 Scope of contract document
3 Specification or statement of requirements
4 Technical drawings (where relevant) with reference, sheet and version number
5 General conditions of contract
6 Special conditions of contract
7 Invitation to tender, tender form and attached schedules
8 Any correspondence referred to in the letter of acceptance.

5   Pre-qualification questionnaires

5.1 A pre-qualification questionnaire (PQQ) is a questionnaire assessing an organisation's commercial, technical and financial capabilities. It provides a method of shortlisting interested suppliers meeting the required minimum qualification criteria.

5.2 A PQQ is used to ascertain the suitability, capacity and capability of potential suppliers. This is a necessary process to ensure that money is spent with capable and stable suppliers. PQQs are very common in the public sector, but are also used in private sector tendering.

5.3 Buyers will use a PQQ to assess the resources and capability of suppliers who express interest in a contract opportunity. This is usually, but not always, done when there is a lot of interest and it is not feasible to invite all interested suppliers to submit a bid. The intention of this stage of the procurement process is to identify the suppliers who are most capable of performing the contract.

5.4 The PQQ will usually be made available to all suppliers that respond to a tender notice and will normally be free of charge. However, in certain tenders a buyer will evaluate the supplier's Expression of Interest (EOI) in order to determine which suppliers should receive the PQQ.

5.5 Typically, PQQs are scored according to the answers given. There may be further bidding, but otherwise the supplier with the best total score will, in most cases, be awarded the contract.

Details of the pre-qualification questionnaire

5.6   PQQs are used to obtain information about potential suppliers and are typically divided into sections such as the following.

- Company details
- Financial information
- Business activities
- References
- Insurance
- Quality assurance
- Health and safety policy
- Equality
- Corporate social responsibility (CSR) policy
- Environmental management policy
- Professional and business standing
- Technical ability

5.7   The buyer will evaluate all PQQs and those suppliers that achieve the required benchmark will be invited to tender.

More detail on the content of PQQs

5.8   In the paragraphs below we look in more detail at the content of a typical PQQ.

5.9   **Supplier's status.** The tendering organisation's registered address, tax registration number, parent company (if applicable), type of organisation (partnership, limited company, consortium etc), contact details of directors and those responsible for managing the tender. If the supplier plans to use subcontractors in the delivery of the contract, details are also required. The supplier must also outline how the organisation is capable to deliver, ideally giving examples of how they have already carried out similar work.

5.10   **Supplier's finances.** An organisation must prove that it is financially sound. The PQQ will require information from recent accounts, such as turnover and current cashflow position. A banker's reference will also be required. The supplier will also be required to have the necessary insurance in place, which will include employer's liability insurance and public liability insurance as a minimum.

5.11   **Quality**. The buyer has to be sure that suppliers chosen have strict quality measures in place to ensure the project is delivered to specification within the required budget and timescale. To provide assurance, suppliers must demonstrate their ability to maintain a high level of quality. As a minimum, an organisation will need a quality assurance policy. Many buyers require more than this. For example, they may require suppliers to have a formal quality management system (QMS) in place, such as ISO 9001 (an externally verified quality accreditation).

5.12   **Environmental standards.** Suppliers are increasingly required to demonstrate their environmental credentials. Generally, an environmental policy is a minimum. However external accreditations such as ISO 14001 provide better evidence of a tendering organisation's commitment to the environment.

5.13   **Equality**. It is important to be aware of legal obligations that local and central government and private companies have in regard to equality. An equality policy will be required, stating how the supplier gives consideration to equality at work.

5.14   **Health and safety**. A health and safety policy will be required. The health and safety accreditation OHSAS 18001 (despite not being an ISO standard) will add support to a supplier's bid.

5.15   **Ability to deliver.** The PQQ will ask how a supplier is best suited for the contract, ideally by giving examples of similar work carried out. References from other customers or clients are expected. The supplier may need to send CVs of the management team or of those employees directly involved in the particular contract.

Following submission

5.16   After the closing date, the buyer will evaluate the submitted PQQs. This can be quite an intensive process often with specialist evaluators used. There should be a date given for the deadline of all PQQs being reviewed. Once reviewed, invitations to tender (ITTs) are then sent to suppliers who have successfully passed the PQQ process.

Chapter summary

- A buyer may invite a supplier to bid for a contract, either with a request for quotation, or with an invitation to tender.
- All quotations and tenders received should be analysed carefully. It is not simply a matter of choosing the lowest quoted price.
- A buyer will often communicate his requirement to suppliers by using a specification. Increasingly, performance specifications are preferred to conformance specifications.
- There are additional difficulties in specifying services.
- Key performance indicators may be used to appraise a supplier's performance.
- Contracts may be based on both express and implied terms.
- Many organisations use standard contracts and/or model form contracts.
- The contract document will typically be supported by a number of schedules.
- A pre-qualification questionnaire is used to assess a potential supplier's commercial, technical and financial capabilities before award of contract.

 ## Self-test questions

Numbers in brackets refer to the paragraphs where you can check your answers.

1   What details are typically included on an RFQ? (1.3)

2   Explain three different approaches to a tendering exercise. (1.11)

3   What are the purposes of a specification? (2.2)

4   Distinguish between a conformance specification and a performance specification. (2.4, 2.6)

5   What are the particular advantages of performance specifications? (2.9)

6   What are the additional difficulties associated with specifying services? (2.12)

7   List benefits of using KPIs to monitor supplier performance. (3.8)

8   List possible KPIs for supplier performance. (Table 2.2)

9   What is meant by an implied term in a contract? (4.4)

10   What is a model form contract? (4.12)

11   List typical contents of a PQQ. (5.6)

CHAPTER 3

Post-Award Administration

Assessment criteria and indicative content

 Explain the administration of the award and post award stages of a sourcing process

- The creation of orders or tender award documentation
- Delivery notes and order acknowledgements
- Receiving invoices
- Invoice matching and dealing with non-compliances

Section headings

1. Purchase orders
2. Tender award documentation
3. Delivery notes and order acknowledgements
4. Dealing with supplier invoices

1 Purchase orders

1.1 A purchase order (PO) is a commercial document issued by a buyer to a seller indicating types, quantities, and agreed prices for products or services the seller will provide to the buyer. Sending a purchase order to a supplier constitutes a legal offer to buy products or services. Acceptance of a purchase order by a seller usually forms a contract between the buyer and seller. A PO is used to control the purchasing of products and services from external suppliers.

1.2 A PO typically contains most or all of the following items of information.

- Title of document (ie *Purchase Order*)
- Name, address and contact details of the buyer
- Serial number and date of the document
- Name and address of the supplier
- Description of item(s) required, with supplier's product codes if known
- Quantity of items required
- Unit price of items required, and total price
- Required delivery date and location
- Shipping instructions
- Payment terms
- The relevant cost centre (ie the department responsible for the requisition)

1.3 The PO needs to satisfy a multitude of purposes and uses. It conveys the requirements of internal users to external suppliers. It must therefore meet the needs both of internal customers and of external suppliers.

1.4 An internal user first completes an internal purchase requisition, as we saw in Chapter 1. In completing this, the internal user must examine the need for the purchase, discuss it with those concerned, secure a budget allocation and determine a cost centre to charge against. This must all be done before Purchasing will raise the PO.

1.5 Key internal information will be transferred from the purchase requisition to the PO. This will include finance information, budget and cost centre details, product description and product numbers, and internal reference details. On computer-based systems the software programme will extract the information from the purchase requisition automatically to complete specific boxes on the PO.

1.6 If Procurement accepts the requisition and raises the PO, more detail will need to be added. The supplier details will be entered either manually or on computer by a short recognition code. This code will pull up all the relevant supplier details: not only the address but also any relevant financial information such as the supplier's tax registration number, applicable discount etc.

1.7 If it is the first time a supplier is being used their details will need to be entered onto the system manually for future use.

1.8 The procurement department will allocate the PO number and record it in the purchase log (manually or electronically). Procurement will add further details relevant to the purchase such as price, delivery terms and payment terms.

1.9 The process will vary from company to company, but the same basic steps are typically taken. The process is essentially the same whether it is a manual or automated system. The difference lies in the speed and sophistication of the operation.

Authorisation

1.10 The completed PO will require authorisation before being sent. This is good business practice and ensures that company policy is being followed. The objective of authorisation is to check that the details are correct, that the purchase order has the correct budget and cost centres, that the delivery and transfer of title aspects are correct and to verify that this is a genuine company purchase.

Despatch procedures

1.11 The completed PO will be printed off and sent by mail. In most cases it will also be sent direct to the supplier by email. In linked computer systems the transfer of the PO will be managed electronically throughout.

1.12 There is often an acknowledgement slip attached for the supplier to annotate (if necessary) and sign. This acceptance makes the contract come into being. With electronic systems the acknowledgement will be returned authorised with an electronic signature from the supplier.

1.13 Copies of the completed order will be required by other departments within the company.

- The person who raised the purchase requisition will require a copy. This enables them to update their file (if held manually) or to see that the file has updated (if the requisition was sent electronically).
- A copy will be sent to the Finance Department. For Finance the PO is one of the key documents enabling payment to be made. (The other documents are the supplier's invoice and the goods received note.)

- Other parties may be interested, eg for reference or statistical purposes, but that will depend on the individual company. With electronic systems the distribution of copies will be managed automatically or by clicking a routing button.

1.14   The details of the PO process naturally vary from company to company. The best way to appreciate raising a PO is to look at the way in which it is managed in your company and, if possible, to discuss with others the processes and approach involved within their procurement department.

Individual POs

1.15   Individual POs are used for one order only and PO numbers are not predefined. Each PO should be listed in a purchase log as an ongoing record, in numerical sequence of the POs issued. The log can be kept manually, on spreadsheet, or as part of an integrated computer system. However it is maintained, the log should contain the PO number, the order status, the supplier's name, a brief description of the goods or services and the total value of the order.

1.16   This purchase log serves as a detailed list and summary of the commitments that one person and/ or the entire department is responsible for.

1.17   In most instances this log is part of a computer-based procurement system, or at the very least a spreadsheet. As part of an integrated system the information held in the purchase log is central to many aspects of the system. It links to areas such as commodity and materials purchases, record of closed orders, supplier records etc, many of which draw much of their data and information from the purchase log.

2   Tender award documentation

2.1   In cases where a purchase is being made following a tender process, the tender award documents fulfil the same purpose as a PO. In this section of the chapter we look at the documentation typically issued following completion of a tendering exercise.

Notification to participants

2.2   All participants in a tender exercise should be notified as soon as possible regarding the outcome of the tender.

Approvals

2.3   In many cases, the decision to award the contract will be taken by an internal Approvals Board who will ensure they are satisfied with the quality of successful tender, that award criteria have been fairly and transparently applied in the judgement, and that appropriate internal and national regulations have been adhered to.

2.4   Use of an Approvals Board will be determined by the value of the contract, or perhaps the political or social importance of the service.

Contract award notice

2.5   As a matter of good practice, successful and unsuccessful bidders must be informed of the decision. The following documents will usually be sent to suppliers who have bid for the contract.

- Award notification letter
- Details of who won the contract
- Anonymous scores of all bidders, and explanation of why the highest bidder scored
- Reasons for the decision

2.6   The award notification should be reviewed carefully to ensure the following details are accurate.

- The award is made to the approved bidder.
- The bidder's name and address details are identical with those under which the offer was made.
- The description of the goods, services or project, and the delivery location, is identical to that quoted in the ITT.
- The contract price shown conforms with the bidder's offer, including any amendments (which should be noted).
- The offer being accepted is correctly identified. If the buyer is accepting options or alternatives he must identify which ones are being accepted.

Award letter

2.7   An award letter is the decision notice sent out to the successful supplier(s) once the evaluation decision has been made. It is important to get this right in order to manage the legal risk of a challenge and to avoid unnecessary delay in the award of the contract.

2.8   Given that the buyer is likely to be entering into contractual relations with the successful bidder, the aim is to draft the award notice in a positive way that gives encouragement and comfort to the successful bidder, while at the same time ensuring that the buyer does not commit itself to any binding legal obligations at this stage. There is still the chance that unsuccessful bidders may challenge the award.

2.9   The buyer should notify the provider that the submitted proposal is the best apparent solution for the project for which the RFQ was issued. The award is not officially definitive as unsuccessful bidders have the right to formally contest their disqualification, rejection, or non-selection within a reasonable time-frame, as initially stated in the RFQ. The buyer should not sign any contract with the provider until the deadline to receive protests expires and all protests are settled.

2.10   The award letters and unsuccessful quotation letters to unsuccessful bidders should all be despatched at the same time.

Implementing new contracts

2.11   Buyer and supplier should meet as soon as possible after the contract has been awarded. The purpose of this meeting is to discuss the contract implementation and to agree roles, responsibilities, activities and timescales. The supplier must be very clear about the criteria that performance will be judged upon and must be confident of being able to meet those criteria.

2.12   It is important for buyer and supplier to be in regular contact during the contract implementation phase and to ensure that expectations are being met.

2.13   Depending on the contract, it may be helpful for the buyer and supplier to create an information pack for any users containing key information about the use of the contract.

- Details of the goods and services available through the contract

- Prices
- Supplier contact details
- Ordering information
- Processes for returns and complaints
- Processes for contract management and supplier management

3 Delivery notes and order acknowledgements

3.1 The PO becomes the template for a number of other documents used in the procurement process, particularly the delivery note and the invoice. We have called the documents discussed here by particular names, eg the consignment note and the delivery note, but they do have other names. In some organisations, for example, the delivery note may be called a packing note and the consignment note may be called a despatch note or a convoy note.

Follow-up of the order

3.2 It is not safe to assume that the transaction is now complete. There will often be a need to follow-up, chase or 'expedite' an order. The buyer may chase the supplier to return the acknowledgement copy of the PO, for example, or to check that the delivery will be on schedule, or to 'track' the progress of the order and its delivery (eg using online 'track and trace' systems, in which each step in the fulfilment of an order, and its transport, is logged for monitoring).

3.3 Usually, these routines are triggered by review of outstanding orders. In some organisations this may mean reference to a manual file or folder of such orders. More often nowadays, POs are logged on a computer system which will automatically flag when follow-up routines are needed.

Order acknowledgement

3.4 This form says 'We have received your order and will meet your requirements except for . . .' This tells the buying organisation what the likely outcome of the purchase will be. First of all it confirms that the supplier has received the order. Hopefully, the supplier will not list any exceptions but sometimes stock shortages might mean the order can't be fulfilled for the time being. For example, if we order ten units, we may be told that eight are in stock and can be delivered immediately, while the remaining two can be supplied a week later.

3.5 When we receive the order acknowledgement we should check it and, if there are no exceptions, file it. However, if there are exceptions we should let our user know. This is because we cannot judge the importance of those exceptions. If we look at our previous example, our user may be quite happy to receive eight of a product as that will last him for four weeks by which time the remaining two will have arrived. On the other hand he may require all ten for an urgent job next week.

3.6 Once we have dealt with any exceptions our supplier will arrange delivery of the goods through the organisation's logistics department. This will be done using a sales order which will detail all the information we included in our PO. Once our order is ready the supplier's logistics department will despatch the goods, accompanied by two further documents: a consignment note and a delivery note.

Consignment note

3.7 This is a document which is used to tell the vehicle driver to deliver a specified number of boxes to a specified address. This document acts as a receipt which confirms that the driver did, in fact, deliver the boxes. However, the consignment note doesn't tell us what is in the boxes and, more importantly, it doesn't guarantee that the goods are in good condition.

3.8 It would be unreasonable for us to delay the driver until we have opened all of the boxes and checked their contents. On the other hand, we don't want anyone to think that, just because we received the boxes, we were happy with their contents. To avoid this we would normally sign for the boxes and endorse the receipt 'Received uninspected'. This allows the driver to leave and allows us to retain the right to go back to our supplier if we find anything amiss.

Delivery note

3.9 This document is very similar to the PO with the addition of the quantity despatched as well as the quantity ordered and it tells us what is in each of the boxes. By checking it against a copy of the PO and the goods actually received we can ascertain whether the delivery is correct or not.

Receiving the goods

3.10 When the goods arrive, it is essential to make sure that the delivery is correct by referring to the contract or PO. The goods will normally arrive accompanied by two documents: a consignment note which says how many boxes the delivery consists of; and a delivery note which says what the boxes contain. If the correct number of boxes has been received, delivery can be accepted but it should be specified that it was 'received uninspected'. This allows the delivery vehicle to leave without waiting for the contents of the boxes to be checked.

3.11 When checking the contents against the PO, things to look out for include the following.

- The part number of each item. If an item cannot be identified – perhaps because the supplier has changed the part number – the goods should be isolated until the matter has been taken up with the supplier.
- The condition of the goods. If there are any damaged or poor quality goods, they should be isolated and the supplier should be informed. In certain circumstances it may be necessary to carry out a more formal and rigorous inspection to ensure that the goods conform to the specification.
- The quantity of the goods. There are two documents involved – the PO and the delivery note – as well as the goods themselves. All three must align if the goods are to be accepted.

3.12 Table 3.1 below indicates the action to be taken in the event of a discrepancy.

Table 3.1 *Checks on delivery of goods*

QUANTITY ORDERED	DELIVERY NOTE QUANTITY	PHYSICAL QUANTITY	ACTION TO TAKE
10	10	10	Receipt correct, book goods into stock
10	3	3	Book 3 into stock, check 7 to follow later
10	10	5	Problem – isolate goods and take the matter up with our supplier
10	10	15	Problem – isolate goods and take the matter up with our supplier
10	15	15	Problem – isolate goods and take the matter up with our supplier
10	15	10	Problem – isolate goods and take the matter up with our supplier
10	5	10	Problem – isolate goods and take the matter up with our supplier
10	15	12	Problem – isolate goods and take the matter up with our supplier

Processing discrepancies and rejections

3.13   There are many cases where the transaction does not flow through exactly as anticipated. For example, the supplier may deliver the wrong goods, or the wrong quantity. Alternatively, there may be a problem with the quality of the goods delivered; this might be detected by the inspection department.

3.14   In all such cases the buyer will need to liaise with the supplier to ensure that the matter is resolved. If this leads to disruption to schedules, or to increased costs of inspection, the buyer will seek financial compensation from the supplier.

Goods received note

3.15   The Goods Inwards department sends a *goods received note* (GRN) to the procurement and finance departments, to indicate that the goods have arrived. This will also note any discrepancies or defects in the order, which the procurement department will need to raise and resolve with the supplier, prior to authorisation of payment.

Closing the transaction

3.16   Once all goods have been received, and the supplier's invoice has been received and checked, it is time to close the transaction. It is usual to do this by noting on the PO the details of goods received documentation showing that the goods ordered have actually been received. Similarly, the order may be annotated to reflect the receipt and vouching of the supplier's invoice.

3.17   Once all this has been done, the order may be filed along with other completed orders.

3.18   It is important to ensure that all files and records relating to POs are maintained in good order. This makes it easier to investigate any queries that arise later. It also gives buyers a permanent record of how a particular order was satisfied. This can be a vital aid in future procurement decisions. For example, if the records show that Supplier X performed badly in supplying Component Z then buyers will not make the mistake of using that supplier again.

3.19   The use of computers greatly simplifies this process of record keeping. In addition, once data has been entered onto a computerised system it is easy to generate reports. For example, it would be a simple matter for a computer to summarise all transactions with a particular supplier, or all transactions relating to a particular part or material. This is a great help to buyers in planning future purchases.

4 Dealing with supplier invoices

4.1 As we have seen, the supplier will in due course send an invoice or request for payment to the buyer. This document will look very similar to the PO and will show us the cost of every product sent or service provided, the delivery charges and any sales tax payable.

4.2 Procurement should check that the invoice corresponds to the order or contract (in regard to the agreed price) and to the GRN (in regard to goods actually received), and then either query discrepancies with the supplier or authorise the invoice for payment and pass it to the accounts department for payment.

4.3 Invoices should be paid within the period stated in the agreed terms of trade: often 30, 60 or 90 days. Credit periods are an issue for cashflow, for both the buyer and the supplier. The buyer may want to pay as late as possible, in order to retain his cash (or earn interest on his banked funds), but the supplier will want to be paid as early as possible, to obtain those same benefits – especially since he has already incurred the cost of supplying the product or service.

4.4 It is part of ethical trading to pay supplier invoices on time, as agreed. It also impacts on the buyer's standing as an attractive (or unattractive) customer for suppliers, and on the ongoing relationship with suppliers. An unjustly unpaid invoice may result in stoppage of supply until the matter is settled, and/or the threat of legal action by the supplier. Repeated late payment or disputed payment of invoices can significantly damage the buyer's credibility, the supplier's loyalty and commitment (and therefore future reliability and quality), and in the worst case, the buyer's ability to find suppliers willing to do business.

4.5 Commercial payments are often made by electronic credit transfer, through the banking system, which is safe and swift. (One disadvantage, however, is that payments tend to be handled on regular days of the month, on a payment cycle, which may represent a late payment for a supplier, or prevent the buyer from receiving an early payment discount.)

4.6 Another possibility is payment by corporate credit card or purchasing card, which allows the delegation of routine purchases to user-department staff, and is efficient in terms of invoicing and other transaction costs. However, this may also allow 'maverick' spending by non-procurement specialists, unless safeguards are in place: eg spending limits on the use of cards, authorised supplier lists and so on.

Dealing with non-compliance on invoices

4.7 The supplier's invoice, the PO and the goods received note provide the three key documents used by IT systems in order to progress an order for payment. But first the buyer must be satisfied that the invoice is compliant in all respects.

4.8 Buyers should ensure that there is a set process and policy in place for handling non-compliant invoices and ensuring they are presented promptly and in the correct formal manner. Particularly in organisations that use e-invoicing as part of an overall procurement system there will be a set procedure to ensure invoices are compliant.

4.9   One area of non-compliance occurs when a PO has not been issued. This could be for a number of reasons. Often a user department will refer to the urgency of the requirement, claiming that there simply was not enough time to wait for generation of a PO.

4.10   Typically, electronic systems will accept invoices only if they carry an official PO. Without this, the invoice will be rejected. Most systems will require a completed non-conformance form to be submitted in these instances.

4.11   Non-compliance can be a major issue, particularly for the Finance Department. Many companies may invoke disciplinary action against employees who repeatedly submit non-compliant invoices. With a systems-based approach to invoicing, the system works at its best when the correct documentation in the correct format is submitted.

4.12   Many organisations will go to great lengths to ensure compliant invoices are submitted. Websites will carry blank invoices and example invoices, emphasising how to complete invoices and what is acceptable and what is not.

4.13   As an example, in order for an invoice to be compliant, it must contain the following information.

- A vendor name. This should be the same as on the PO.
- A vendor address.
- A unique invoice number (a unique number prevents the risk of accidental duplicate payment).
- An invoice date.
- Amount and currency.
- Totals must add up correctly.
- Description of goods or services supplied.
- The words 'Invoice' or 'Credit Note', as appropriate.
- A PO number.
- The name of the supplier contact and their telephone extension.

4.14   Non-compliant invoices are expensive and time-consuming to deal with and defeat the purpose of having an integrated approach to invoicing. With IT-based systems there needs to be a rigour in the manner in which non-compliance is handled both with internal staff and external suppliers.

Chapter summary

- A purchase order is issued by a buyer to a supplier indicating what the buyer wishes to purchase.
- In cases where a purchase is being made following a tender process, the tender award documents fulfil the same purpose as a PO.
- Documents in the later stages of the procurement cycle include order acknowledgement, consignment note, delivery note and goods received note.
- Before paying a supplier's invoice, it is important to check that it agrees both with the purchase order and with the goods received note.

 **Self-test questions**

Numbers in brackets refer to the paragraphs where you can check your answers.

1   List details typically contained on a purchase order. (1.2)

2   Who will need copies of the purchase order? (1.13)

3   What documents will usually be sent to suppliers who have bid for a contract in response to a tendering process? (2.5)

4   What is the main message of an order acknowledgement? (3.4)

5   What is a consignment note? (3.7)

6   What is a goods received note? (3.15)

7   What checks should Procurement carry out before approving a supplier's invoice. (4.2)

8   Why might a purchase order not be issued for a particular requirement? (4.9)

CHAPTER 4

The Need for Approvals

Assessment criteria and indicative content

 Describe the need for approvals in the administration of procurement and supply

- Typical procedures for authorising budgets, requisitions, orders and tenders
- The separation of duties
- Contract recommendation and authorisation
- Levels of delegated authority for contracts
- Ensuring an efficient approval process

Section headings

1   Procedures for authorisation
2   The separation of duties
3   Levels of delegated authority for contracts
4   Ensuring an efficient approval process

1   Procedures for authorisation

Authorisation of expenditure

1.1   An important aspect of organisational control is to ensure that activities are properly authorised. This means that actions are not taken unless they have been approved by a staff member of an appropriate level. The level of authorisation required varies, depending largely on the size of the transaction involved.

1.2   The illustrative example in Table 4.1 shows persons authorised to commit the organisation to the purchase of goods and services and to authorise the payment for such goods and services. The figures given are for illustration only; in practice, these might vary widely from one organisation to another.

Table 4.1 *Illustrative hierarchy of authorisation*

EXPENDITURE LEVEL	JOB TITLE/FUNCTION
Over $100,000	Board of Directors
Over $25,000	Finance Director
Over $5,000	Departmental Head
Up to $5,000	Procurement Managers
Up to $1,000	Procurement Officer

Authorisation for budgets

1.3　Budgeting can be defined as 'the act of quantifying objectives in financial terms'. Budgeting performs three main functions in an organisation.

- Quantification of plans
- Help in financial planning
- Monitoring and controlling resources through performance measurement

1.4　Authorisation to spend the organisation's funds is allocated to budget holders. A budget holder is the person authorised to spend a particular allocation of funds. For example, a director of marketing might be the budget holder for all sums of money to be spent on marketing activities.

1.5　A budget holder's responsibilities will vary according to the organisation but its outline will follow the example below.

- Budget holders must control income and expenditure within an agreed allocation. Budget holders must ensure that day-to-day monitoring is undertaken effectively.
- Budget holders are responsible to the Finance Director for the income and expenditure appropriate to their budget allocations.
- Budget holders must ensure that funds are only used for the purpose for which they have been allocated.
- Where variances have been identified, these must be investigated and where appropriate the necessary corrective action must be undertaken. (A variance means an instance where the actual expenditure differs from the budgeted expenditure.)
- The Finance Director must be kept up-to-date on any potential overspends or underspends, as soon as they become apparent.

Authorisation and coding

1.6　Budget holders are responsible for ensuring that all expenditure within their remit is correctly coded so that it can be identified in the accounting system. Procurement is a department that holds considerable responsibility for spend. The department must ensure that all purchases are correctly coded to the requisitioning department. Procedures must be in place to ensure budget details (such as budget codes, cost centres etc) are correctly identified on the accounting system and allocated to the appropriate purchase order.

1.7　The purchase order together with the supplier's invoice and the goods received note are the three key documents that enable the Finance Department to progress the order for payment.

1.8　When an invoice has been processed by the finance operation there is usually a requirement for internal budget holders to approve the purchase invoice for payment and/or to allocate to particular budgets. Internal operations can benefit from using an electronic authorisation process where an email can be sent to the appropriate person indicating they have a task to complete. The link in the email will provide detail and present a copy of the invoice and relevant support information allowing the authorised person to input the required budget codes and authorise or query.

1.9　Once given final approval, the data can be automatically imported into the computer system to update the status of the purchase invoice.

Authorisation for requisitions

1.10   It is normal for the user department concerned to issue a purchase requisition. This form describes the item needed and instigates action by the procurement department. Typically, the originator of the requisition would keep a copy of the form while the other copy is forwarded as appropriate.

- If the originator is the stores department, the copy is forwarded to Procurement for action.
- If the originator is a user department, the copy is forwarded to Stores. Stores will meet the need if the item is in stock, and if not will pass the copy on to Procurement.

1.11   While buyers can use their experience to question requisitions, in the last resort the user department has the most detailed knowledge of their own requirements. This means that care must be taken to avoid inappropriate or irresponsible requisitions.

1.12   When a requisition is originated it must be signed by an authorised individual to whom the budget-holder (and not the buyer) is responsible before being passed to Procurement. This gives procurement the assurance they need that the requisition is for an item that is genuinely needed.

1.13   In many cases it will be appropriate to refer the requisition back to the originator. This may simply be for clarification if the requisition is unclear, but may also be to suggest alternatives that offer better quality or lower price than the item specified. Procurement should not make such changes without consultation because they cannot know all the factors that the originator may have had in mind when drawing up the requisition. But neither should they accept requisitions without question.

Authorisation for orders

1.14   Buyers will often signal a requirement to suppliers by preparation of a specification. It is advisable to ensure controlled **signing-off procedures**. Before a specification is released to a supplier it must have the formal approval of the procurement department and ideally the prior certification of the supplier. This reduces the common risk of changes being made in order to solve problems not envisaged at the time the specification was finalised.

1.15   This precaution should then be followed up by ensuring that any changes which *are* deemed necessary are subjected to appropriate approval procedures – in writing.

1.16   The authorisation hierarchy within the procurement department will ensure that all orders above a specified level are viewed and approved by at least two people. This approach adds rigour to the order placing process and reduces the likelihood of fraud occurring.

1.17   Procurement must ensure that all information is correct and all budgeting requirements have been met before progressing the order through to placement.

Authorisation for tenders

1.18   For larger purchases, it may be appropriate to go through a full tendering procedure. In the public sector, this is often compulsory for purchases above a defined (low) threshold. Public sector tenders are highly regulated and the process involved highly structured to demonstrate fairness, equality and rigour.

1.19   Table 4.2 shows an illustrative hierarchy of purchases, based on the amount of money involved.

The figures are purely illustrative and for any particular organisation the amounts may differ.

Table 4.2 *A hierarchy of purchases*

VALUE OF PURCHASES	MINIMUM REQUIREMENT
Over $50,000	Full open tender
$10,001 to $50,000	Selective tender
$5,001 to $10,000	At least three written quotes
$1,001 to $5,000	At least two written quotes
Up to $1,000	Budget holder judgement

1.20 Public sector bodies may set out a **scheme of delegation** which sets out (for example) four levels of authorisation of delegated authority limits.

1.21 Each of these parties can sign to specific levels. However, if those limits are exceeded, two or more signatories may be required. This is to protect public funds and guard against fraud. Robust systems also protect staff against any suspicion of financial impropriety.

2 The separation of duties

2.1 The separation of duties is an internal control concept that requires different people to complete different parts of a task. One objective is to prevent a single person from defrauding the organisation. Another is to catch and prevent serious errors from occurring.

2.2 The concept of separation of duties can be difficult to achieve while maximising efficiencies. The organisation will have to measure the trade-off of an efficient process against the risk of a fraudulent employee going undetected.

2.3 As an example, the separation of duties requires that the person responsible for balancing the monthly payroll must be different from the person issuing the payroll payments. If a single person performed all of these duties there would be a danger of errors or fraud.

2.4 The separation of duties is one of several steps to improve the internal control of an organisation's assets. For example, the internal control of cash is improved if the money handling duties are separated from the record keeping duties. Separating these duties means that the likelihood of theft is reduced because it will now require two dishonest people working together to admit to each other that they are dishonest, plan the theft, and to then carry out the theft. One person will have to remove the cash and the other person will have to falsify the records.

2.5 Without the separation of duties, the theft of cash is easier. One dishonest person can steal the money *and* enter a fictitious amount into the records – thereby concealing the theft.

2.6 Other steps in improving internal control over cash are to use a cash register, to issue receipts, and to have two people present when cash is handled.

2.7 The basic principle for separation of duties is that the person approving an action, the person carrying out the action, and the person monitoring the action must be separate. The goal is to eliminate the possibility of a single user from carrying out and concealing a prohibited action. By separating the authorisation, implementation and monitoring roles, fraud can only be successfully carried out through the collusion of multiple parties. This makes it much less likely that fraud will occur.

2.8   Separation of duties is a fundamental security principle. It ensures that a single person does not have the ability to abuse their powers or make significant errors. The general principle is that collusion between a number of people is required to abuse the process. No single person should have the authority to cause damage acting on his or her own.

Separation of duties in procurement

2.9   In procurement, duties should be divided between two or more people in order that no one person is responsible for the entire procurement process. The process involves three key authorities.

- Budget holder authority
- Authority to seek quotations and commit
- Authority to accept quotations and pay invoices

2.10   It is important to identify all the potential risk and control points in the procurement process and to decide what, if any, controls should exist. The assessment should include both financial and non-financial risks (eg reputational risk). It is prudent to carry out an appropriate cost-benefit analysis to ensure any measures are seen as cost-effective.

2.11   There are many control points in the separation of duties. CIPS summarises them in broad terms as follows.

- Requisition and specification: who authorises the requisition and who authorises the specification?
- Supplier selection process: who draws up tender lists, organises the receipt of tenders, produces shortlists, and undertakes negotiation?
- Contract award: who decides on the successful supplier, and who authorises the contract or purchase order?
- Goods received: who checks that what has been ordered and what will be paid for has actually been received?
- Payment process: who authorises the payment (signs off the invoice and arranges payment)?

2.12   CIPS believes that it is good practice for a minimum of two different employees to be responsible for the following sequence of three activities from the previous list.

- Determining the need (eg the requisition or specification)
- Undertaking the procurement (eg sourcing and commitment)
- Effecting the financial aspects (eg authorising payment)

2.13   Some organisations use a table of delegations of authority setting out who has the authority to approve what. In some organisations many people may hold responsibility for the three roles but no single individual should have responsibility for more than one of the roles. The main reason for allocating different duties to different employees is that a single individual is not able to influence the outcome to their advantage.

3 Levels of delegated authority for contracts

Definitions

3.1 A manager cannot personally perform all the tasks assigned to him. In order to meet targets, the manager needs to delegate authority. Delegation of authority means division of authority and powers downwards to a subordinate. Delegation is about trusting someone else to do parts of your job.

3.2 It is useful to have some definitions.

- Authority is the right to exercise power in a particular context.
- Delegation is the process by which a person or group possessing authority transfers part of that authority to another person or group.
- Responsibility is the obligation to use delegated powers appropriately.
- Accountability is the liability of each person who is given authority to give an account of their use of that authority (ie their performance) to the person who delegated it to them.

3.3 As an example, a managing director might direct a procurement manager to award a contract for a particular project. The managing director has used his authority to delegate the responsibility to the procurement manager. The procurement manager is now accountable to the managing director for the successful outcome.

Contract recommendation and authorisation

3.4 The procurement manager will now decide how to accomplish the task delegated by the managing director.

3.5 The delegation of authority is the basis of superior-subordinate relationship. It involves the following steps.

- The assignment of duties. This is accomplished by defining the task and duties to the subordinate together with the result expected from the subordinate. Clarity of duty as well as result expected has to be the first step in delegation.
- The granting of authority. The subdivision of authority takes place when the procurement manager (as a superior) divides and shares his authority with his staff. Every subordinate should be given enough independence to carry out the task given to him by his superiors. Managers at all levels delegate authority and power which is attached to their job positions. The subdivision of powers is very important to get effective results.
- Creating responsibility and accountability. The delegation process does not end once powers are granted to the subordinates. They at the same time may need to delegate specific areas of the proposed contact to their staff. The staff, in turn have the responsibility to carry out the duties to the best of their ability in line with the directions of the superior.

3.6 Through delegation, the procurement manager increases the amount he is able to achieve by dividing his work with his subordinates. For example different individuals could be tasked with sending out the invitations to tender, arranging bid evaluation, and establishing contact management after the contract has been awarded.

4 Ensuring an efficient approval process

4.1 Within procurement it is necessary for someone in a more senior position to authorise the purchase decision of a subordinate. It may be that certain products or spend limits are automatically authorised but generally it is considered good practice to ensure purchase decisions are approved by a more senior person or by a specialist.

4.2 By allowing individuals to authorise certain levels of spend without requiring the approval of a person senior in the organisation a high degree of control is introduced and risk is reduced.

4.3 Decisions made will usually require some form of authorisation before they are allowed to proceed. Depending on the size and complexity of the organisation this process can become highly involved and in consequence developing an approval hierarchy underpins an efficient approval process.

Approval hierarchy

4.4 An approval hierarchy is a private hierarchy within an organisation that allows authorised individuals to approve purchase and financial transactions.

4.5 An approval hierarchy will contain various approval levels that funnel transaction approval up through an approval chain. At each level the authorised individual can approve or reject the submitted transaction.

4.6 Here is an example of how it works. In this example the Senior Manager is the manager of the Junior Buyer and the Group Manager is the manager of the Senior Manager.

EMPLOYEE	IS MANAGED BY	APPROVAL LIMIT
Junior Buyer	Senior Manager	$500.00
Senior Manager	Group Manager	$1,000.00
Group Manager		Unlimited

- The Junior Buyer raises a purchase order that has a total value of $1,500.00.
- The purchase order is submitted for approval.
- As the Junior Buyer does not have high enough approval limits, the purchase order is automatically forwarded to the Senior Manager (as the Senior Manager is the Junior Buyer's supervisor as defined in the hierarchy).
- The Senior Manager responds to the approval notification for this purchase order.
- If the Senior Manager selects 'Approve' the purchase order is automatically forwarded to the Group Manager as the Senior Manager does not have a high enough approval limit.
- The purchase order appears on the notification screen for the Group Manager where it can be approved or rejected.

Authorisation and coding

4.7 When an invoice has been processed by the finance operation there is usually a requirement for internal budget holders to approve the purchase invoice for payment and/or to allocate to particular budgets. Internal operations can benefit from using an electronic authorisation process where an email can be sent to the appropriate person indicating they have a task to complete.

The link in the email will provide detail and present a copy of the invoice and relevant support information allowing the authorised person to input the required budget codes and authorise or query.

4.8   Once given final approval, the data can be automatically imported into the computer system to update the status of the purchase invoice.

Automating requisitions, purchase orders and invoices

4.9   A computerised procurement system can introduce efficiency controls. As an example, the software can cross-reference procurement budgets to ensure compliance with pre-determined buying limits. A requisition that was within the defined limit would be routed for approval, converted into a purchase order once approved, and immediately sent to the correct supplier by email.

4.10   The automation of the procurement process can lead to better financial controls, lower production costs, reduced overheads and better and more efficient relationships with operations staff and suppliers.

4.11   Automated controls can cover cross-referencing procurement budgets with pre-defined buying limits, ensuring that approval limits are met before progressing the order, and ensuring that product specifications are consistent throughout the purchase cycle.

Resolving queries and anomalies

4.12   To ensure procurement timescales are being met it is necessary to incorporate a hierarchy to ensure queries and anomalies are dealt with promptly and efficiently. Identified anomalies are emailed to the relevant approver for resolution. The nominated approver can then forward, hold, reject or approve the invoice. Many systems will send email alerts with automatic escalations built in to ensure that the anomaly is quickly dealt with, and invoices or queries do not get lost in approvers' in-trays.

4.13   The system places pressure on the approver to resolve the situation in a timely manner by recording the time of the original notification and automatically escalating the query perhaps to remind the approver or to advise the next person higher up the hierarchy that a query still exists after a set time.

4.14   In certain cases it may be prudent to have a person outside the hierarchy to review the situation. A reviewer is an individual outside the approver's hierarchy to whom a requisition or anomaly has been forwarded for review. A reviewer does not have any approval authority. Instead their views will be recorded in the approval history with their review comments only.

4.15   Getting the basics right consistently is important. After the goods are received the invoice needs to be reconciled to the purchase order and goods receipt before payment is made. Are the charges for the right goods and services? Are the amounts the contracted amounts? Were the quantities correct? Are any other charges, including taxes, valid and correct? Within an organisation place emphasis on resolving issues within a stated time-frame and ensure this is adhered to or there are known reasons why the issue remains unresolved.

Chapter summary

- An important aspect of organisational control is to ensure that activities (especially expenditure) are properly authorised.
- Control over expenditure is usually effected by means of a system of budgeting. Specific levels of funding are allocated to defined budget holders.
- Another key aspect of internal control is separation of duties. The person approving an action, the person carrying out the action, and the person monitoring the action must all be distinct.
- A manager can achieve more by delegating some of his authority to subordinates.
- Purchase decisions should be supported by an approval hierarchy. The higher the level of expenditure, the more senior must be the person authorising it.

Self-test questions

Numbers in brackets refer to the paragraphs where you can check your answers.

1   What are the three main functions of budgeting? (1.3)

2   List responsibilities of a budget holder. (1.5)

3   What is the purpose of separation of duties? (2.1)

4   List points in the procurement cycle where CIPS identify a need for control. (2.11)

5   Define (a) authority and (b) delegation. (3.2)

6   Explain how an approval hierarchy works. (4.4–4.6)

7   What are the advantages of automating procurement processes? (4.10)

CHAPTER 5

Direct and Indirect Supplies

Assessment criteria and indicative content

 Describe what is meant by direct and indirect supplies

- Definitions of direct and indirect supplies
- Examples of direct and indirect supplies
- Goods for resale and goods not for resale

Section headings

1 The nature of direct and indirect supplies
2 Examples of direct and indirect supplies
3 Goods for resale and goods not for resale

1   The nature of direct and indirect supplies

The distinction between direct and indirect procurement

1.1   A manufacturing business generates a constant requirement for production materials. These may take various forms: raw materials, parts and components, subassemblies and so on. Without adequate supplies of these materials when they are needed production operations may be disrupted with expensive consequences. The purchase of these items is often referred to as **direct procurement**.

1.2   Manufacturing businesses also require consumable supplies, sometimes referred to as maintenance, repair and operating (MRO) supplies. And all businesses spend money on general 'running' expenses: travel, stationery, telecommunications etc. The purchase of these items is often referred to as **indirect procurement**.

1.3   In the procurement literature, this distinction is often made in the context of manufacturing businesses alone. However, as procurement disciplines develop and spread more widely in the non-manufacturing sector the distinction is broadened. Nowadays, it is usual to speak of direct procurement when the items purchased are either for resale (eg the goods purchased by a retailer), or for incorporation in goods for sale (eg raw materials purchased by a manufacturer). Indirect procurement then refers to the purchase of any other items. In general, indirect procurement is more likely than direct procurement to be carried out by end users rather than specialist procurement staff.

Porter's value chain model

1.4   A slightly different (but overlapping) way of looking at the distinction between direct and indirect procurement is provided by Professor Michael Porter's value chain model. See Figure 5.1.

Figure 5.1 *Porter's value chain*

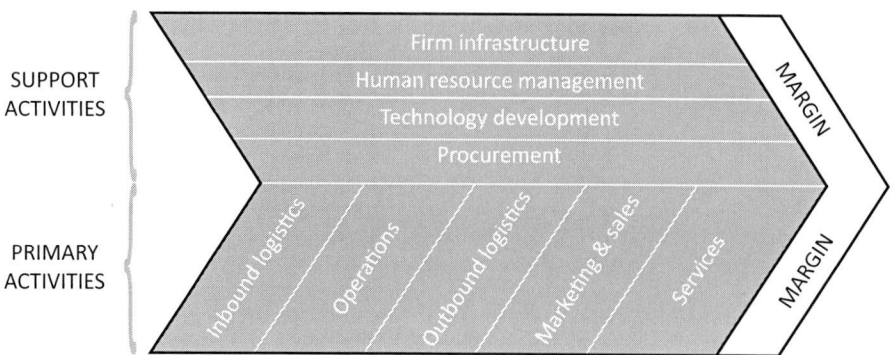

1.5 This model distinguishes between the primary activities of an organisation and the secondary or support activities.

- Primary activities are concerned with bringing resources into the organisation, transforming them by means of a 'production' process, moving finished products to customers, and marketing them.
- Secondary activities are concerned with supporting the primary business functions.

1.6 On this analysis, we use the term direct procurement when we refer to purchases for the primary activities. We use the term indirect procurement to refer to purchases for the support activities. In effect, we are distinguishing between two supply chains: a primary one and a secondary one.

The impact of direct procurement

1.7 We can distinguish certain characteristics that apply to direct procurement.

1.8 The cost of direct purchases is part of the organisation's cost of goods sold. If this can be reduced, the company's gross profit (and as a consequence net profit) will be improved. By contrast, the cost of indirect purchases affects the organisation's overheads. If this can be reduced, net profit will be improved, but there will not be any effect on gross profit.

1.9 The quality of direct purchases has a direct impact on the quality of goods produced. Poor quality will lead to increased quality costs, increased waste, scrap and rejects, and possibly reduced customer satisfaction. By contrast, the quality of indirect purchases does not impact on the production process.

1.10 Direct purchases frequently need to be stocked, so as to ensure there is no disruption to production operations. By contrast, indirect purchases are usually made when required, without holding stocks.

1.11 In terms of supplier relations, direct purchases are more likely to be covered by long-term relationships. By contrast, indirect purchases are frequently made on the basis of one-off, transactional relationships.

1.12 In many organisations, and especially manufacturers, the cost of direct purchases is a very high proportion of total external spend. Opportunities for the procurement function to improve the bottom-line profit are that much greater.

1.13 For example, if a manufacturing company's cost of sales is 60% of its sales revenue (ie it makes a gross profit of 40%), and Procurement can trim 2% from the cost of direct purchases, this translates into a 1.2% increase in gross and net profit. The same organisation might typically spend perhaps 10% of its revenue on indirect purchases; the opportunity for Procurement to improve bottom-line profit in this area is only one-sixth of what it is in the case of direct purchases.

2 Examples of direct and indirect supplies

Direct supplies – production materials for manufacturing

2.1 As we have already said, the distinction between direct and indirect supplies is usually applied in the manufacturing context. Materials used in manufacturing are an example of direct supplies. They are often classified under the three headings of raw materials, components and assemblies, and work in progress.

2.2 **Raw materials** include items extracted from the ground, such as minerals, ores and petroleum. The term also includes agricultural and forestry products: dairy products, fruit, vegetables, timber etc. Often these are sold to manufacturers in an unprocessed state, though in some cases a degree of processing may already have taken place before the manufacturer receives them.

2.3 Manufacturers also purchase **components and assemblies**, which are the finished output of other manufacturers upstream in the supply chain. The buying organisation will wish to incorporate these items as part of their own outputs. There is a modern trend towards purchasing more assemblies, thus taking advantage of suppliers' expertise. This leaves the final manufacturer with less work to do in producing his final output. In earlier decades the final manufacturer would have minimised purchases from outside, preferring instead to perform all manufacture in-house.

2.4 **Work in progress** refers to part-finished output on which the manufacturer has already begun work but which is not yet ready for sale to customers.

2.5 The origins of the procurement and supply profession lie in the manufacturing sector, and consequently procurement disciplines tend to be most highly developed in this sector. Failure to obtain timely and secure supply of high-quality production materials can lead to disruption in the manufacturing operations. The role of procurement and supply is therefore critical.

2.6 A particular problem with many raw materials (eg commodities such as metals, or crops) is that they are subject to very volatile prices. It is important for buyers to monitor relevant factors very carefully: these can include weather conditions, natural disasters, political instability etc. Often a solution may be to adopt a policy of forward buying, which means that buyers deliberately overstock in order to take advantage of a low price. If prices then rise, the existing stocks make it unnecessary to purchase until conditions become more favourable. Of course, the benefits of this policy must be weighed against the costs of storing and insuring the additional stock.

2.7 Here are some of the considerations that buyers must bear in mind in relation to production materials.

- The 'make or buy' decision: to what extent should we manufacture internally, as opposed to sourcing from outside? We have already mentioned that the modern trend has been towards reducing the amount of internal manufacture.

- Buyers must liaise with many internal departments (such as design, engineering etc) in order to produce a specification for the products required. This is of course in addition to liaison with potential suppliers.
- There may be particular issues to negotiate with suppliers, eg the cost of developing specialised tooling to produce the items required.

Indirect supplies – maintenance, repair and operating (MRO) supplies

2.8 MRO supplies have been defined as 'all goods and services (other than capital equipment) necessary to transform raw materials and components into end products'. They include such items as paint, lubricants, packing materials, cleaning products and industrial clothing.

2.9 All manufacturing plants use MRO supplies regularly. The number of MRO items may be very large; some estimates suggest that a moderately large manufacturing plant will carry in excess of 10,000 MRO stock lines. Although usage of any particular part may be relatively slight, the potential for incurring high purchase and stocking costs is clearly high.

2.10 For this reason it is important that procurement staff exercise as disciplined an approach to MRO supplies as to any other area of their responsibilities. This is not always easy to do. One problem is that some firms, failing to recognise the importance of this area, have no defined policy on the issue. Often it is open to user departments to order MRO items without recourse to procurement specialists and with little control over their expenditure.

2.11 The problems associated with MRO items are not all to do with expenditure. Potential disruption to production is an equally important concern. The value of an item may not be fully reflected in its purchase price. If its absence means a production hold-up then it would be more appropriate to measure its value in terms of the additional costs or lost revenue that might result from a stockout.

3 Goods for resale and goods not for resale

Similarities and differences

3.1 In this section we look at the work of buyers employed by wholesalers and retailers. The task of such buyers is to purchase goods which will then be sold onwards to customers with little or no work having been done to them in the meantime. This contrasts with a manufacturing environment, in which buyers purchase materials that will be converted into finished products.

3.2 It should be obvious that important principles of procurement are as relevant here as they are in manufacturing environments. For example, modern approaches to quality assurance, stock control and supplier relations remain vital. Even so, the nature of the work is different in important respects, and the objective here is to isolate these differences and discuss their impact for buyers.

3.3 The most crucial difference is that buyers in resale environments are usually much closer to their (external) customers than is common in manufacturing. This is because the decision on what to buy is crucially related to expectations of what will sell. There is pressure on buyers in this sector to find new lines that will entice additional customers and generate additional income. This is very different from the situation in manufacturing and suggests that an important part of the buyer's training should be in marketing and selling.

3.4   The importance of these distinctions should not be exaggerated. For one thing, the similarities between procurement activities in different sectors probably always outweigh the specific differences. Some specific differences are being eroded as procurement disciplines evolve towards a world class standard.

3.5   An example of this is the question of supplier relations. As Arjen van Weele points out, these have typically been less durable in resale than in manufacturing. However, there is a definite trend towards closer and more lasting relationships. One way in which this is evidenced is in the closer involvement of some retailers in the production procedures of manufacturers.

3.6   Partly this is a matter of quality assurance. A retailer wishes to be able to talk with confidence to his customers about the quality of the goods he offers for sale. This is best achieved by working closely with his suppliers, and this implies long-term relations.

3.7   Partly also it reflects the situation where the distinction between supplier and retailer is vague, as has historically been the case with Marks & Spencer in the UK. Marks & Spencer sell their own branded items and their suppliers act, in effect, as the manufacturing arm of the company. For this reason, it is very well known that particularly close relations have existed between M&S and their suppliers. Baily, Farmer, Jessop and Jones (in *Procurement Principles and Management*) state that M&S have sometimes been called 'a manufacturer without factories'.

3.8   Where an organisation sells 'own-label' products, the role of the retail buyer becomes much more similar to that of the industrial buyer. In each case, procurement aims to get from the supplier a product which matches the buyer's specification.

3.9   Often a producer will produce both their own branded goods (for sale at a premium price) and equivalent non-branded goods (sometimes referred to as **white label goods**). These latter will be sold to supermarkets who want to apply their own branding. From the producer's point of view, this maximises revenue by satisfying all sectors of the market. The discounted price is affordable to the supplier because the white label version will usually be of lower quality and cheaper to produce.

3.10   A number of issues are increasingly subject to debate among buyers and suppliers.

- Buyers may seek to encourage standardisation and variety reduction among manufacturers.
- Buyers may put pressure on manufacturers to provide training to personnel handling their goods.
- Buyers may look to suppliers for a contribution to advertising costs to the extent that this is likely to benefit the supplier.

The importance of technology

3.11   Technological developments have left few areas of business untouched, but their impact on retailing has been particularly dramatic. Improvements in production technology have led to shorter product lifecycles (ie more rapid introduction of new products) which places increased burdens on the retail buyer to stay abreast of events. One step to this end has been greater involvement of buyers in the product development process.

3.12   Purchase ordering is streamlined to suit the fast turnover that is common in resale organisations. Frequent deliveries are essential, which means that ordering procedures must be simple and rapid. Invariably, advanced information technology is used, including **electronic data interchange** (EDI) linking buyers' ordering systems to suppliers' sales systems.

3.13   Once goods are delivered to retail outlets or distribution centres they are recorded in the inventory control system. Many retailers have highly automated systems under which suppliers' performance levels are evaluated at this point in relation to on-time delivery and quality.

3.14   Another important aspect of information technology is the facility it gives to obtain and analyse information about buying patterns among consumers, especially by the use of EPOS systems (electronic point of sale). This is vital for marketing staff in planning prices and promotions and in assessing potential demand for new products. Equally, it gives important clues to buyers as to which products are likely to sell and therefore which products should be bought.

The role of the retail buyer

3.15   The above discussion should have made it clear that buyers in the retail sector may become involved in many different aspects of the business, some of them not conventionally regarded as part of the procurement function at all.

3.16   For example, buyers may become involved in market research activity, partly to establish what their customers wish to buy but also to monitor the activities of competitors. Statistics provided by suppliers are an important source of this kind of information, but should be treated with caution: suppliers have a vested interest in presenting a picture that will promote sales of their products.

3.17   Buyers should also be involved in the process of setting expenditure budgets. This process involves every layer of an organisation, from the very top down to the lowest levels of managerial control. Within a framework laid down by overall organisational budgets individual buyers must negotiate their own spending limits, and other targets such as sales volume and profit margin to be achieved on particular products for which they are responsible.

3.18   Clearly a major part of the buyer's role is in the selection of products and suppliers. Cooperation with other functional areas such as marketing and merchandising is important in this field. Key decision variables obviously include purchase cost (including discounts and trade credit), but buyers will also be influenced by reliability of supply, the extent to which suppliers invest in new product development, and the level of marketing support given. Marketing support could range from high-profile advertising by the manufacturer to provision of ready-to-sell packaging for point of sale promotional material.

3.19   Buyers are also involved in the management of physical inventory, including storage and distribution. It may or may not be appropriate to use the buying firm's own storage facilities. Often in retail contexts it is **not** appropriate, and a mix of just in time principles and storage at suppliers' premises enables buyers to minimise stock held.

3.20   As already explained, an important part of buying is selling. This is the test of whether the buyer has bought well, and the buyer has an obvious interest in becoming involved in this area.

3.21   A common example is the involvement of buyers in sales promotions; where promotions take place the buyer must be alert to the need for additional ordering to meet the expected increase in demand. For consumers, it is frustrating and a source of ill feeling towards the supplier and stockist if a product advertised and promoted strongly is not available for purchase.

3.22   Buyers are involved in monitoring the sales performance of their products. In many retail organisations the responsibilities of buyers include a certain amount of direct communication with suppliers. In other cases, the centralised nature of the procurement function makes such communication less feasible. However this may be, it is clearly essential that a buyer monitors sales figures produced by the information system.

3.23   Finally, buyers must be concerned with evaluation of suppliers. Often they will be aided by computer-produced statistics relating to quality and on-time delivery.

Retail supply chains

3.24   The distinctive feature of retail supply chains is the direct relationship between the retailer and the final consumer. Buyers have to identify new lines that will entice additional customers and demand – which requires marketing-oriented competencies in addition to procurement competencies. Supply chain management will be focused on securing the timely availability or fulfilment of a wide variety of products in response to customer demand.

3.25   Various forms of collaboration have been an increasing feature of retail buyer-supplier relationships, including training of retail sales and service staff by manufacturers, and supplier contribution to retailers' advertising and display costs (where this is of benefit to the supplier). Technological integration has also become widespread, in the form of EDI procurement, automated inventory control and replenishment, and demand management via electronic point of sale (EPOS) systems.

Chapter summary

- Direct purchases are production materials used in manufacturing. Indirect purchases are anything else. It is difficult to make this distinction in non-manufacturing contexts.
- In a typical case, procurement's ability to improve the organisation's profitability is much greater in dealing with direct purchases than with indirect purchases.
- Production supplies can include raw materials, components and assemblies.
- Work in progress is part-finished output not yet ready for supply to customers.
- MRO supplies are all goods and services (other than capital equipment) necessary to transform raw materials and components into end products.
- A key feature of procurement in the retail sector is the close link between procurement and selling.

 **Self-test questions**

Numbers in brackets refer to the paragraphs where you can check your answers.

1   Distinguish between direct and indirect procurement. (1.1, 1.2)

2   List the primary and secondary activities in Porter's value chain. (Figure 5.1)

3   What considerations must buyers bear in mind in relation to production materials? (2.7)

4   What are the particular problems relating to procurement of MRO supplies? (2.11)

5   How do buyer-supplier relations typically differ in retail environments as compared with manufacturing? (3.1–3.10)

6   Explain the importance of technology in the retail environment. (3.11–3.14)

7   Explain the role of the retail buyer. (3.15–3.23)

CHAPTER 6

The Costs of Holding Inventories

Assessment criteria and indicative content

 Identify the key costs associated with holding inventories
- Analysing the costs of inventory
- The costs associated with stockouts and excess inventories

Chapter headings

1 Costs associated with stockouts
2 The costs of acquiring inventories
3 The costs of excess inventories

1 Costs associated with stockouts

1.1 A task facing procurement specialists, working in close co-operation with production, marketing and other functions, is to balance (or better still to reconcile) conflicting demands relating to inventory levels. On the one hand, holding large levels of stock has a cost which must be minimised. On the other hand, very low levels of stock can lead to disruption of production, late deliveries to customers and other problems. In this chapter we look at how procurement staff can approach this dilemma and how we can measure their success in dealing with it.

Safety stocks

1.2 If you look at the balance sheet of a typical manufacturing company you will find that one of the largest monetary amounts in the assets section is the value of stocks. More often than not, the only larger amount is the value of fixed assets: factory, warehouse and office buildings, plant and machinery, motor vehicles etc. Published accounts analyse the total stock figure into its constituent parts, such as stocks of raw materials and consumables, work in progress, finished goods and goods held for resale.

1.3 The level of stockholding in non-manufacturing companies may be less significant, but should not be underestimated. Retailers, for example, will also hold huge levels of stock. It is only in 'pure' service organisations (such as insurance companies or consultancies) that the level of physical stocks is not a major balance sheet element.

1.4 In this first section we look at some of the reasons why firms wish to hold such large stocks. One important reason that occurs immediately is that stockholdings can represent a safety measure. Production scheduling is a difficult matter. Unforeseen events can force production managers to rearrange their plans. This can lead to serious costs in the form of idle time and lost production unless resources can be redeployed quickly.

1.5 Sizeable stocks are often a great help in these circumstances. For example, if procurement staff experience a problem in sourcing a material (perhaps because of the unexpected failure of a supplier) the situation is not too desperate if stocks of that material are already on hand. While the available stocks are being used, procurement have time to find an alternative source.

1.6   This example relates to the beginning of the production line, but the same principle applies at later stages. Suppose that finished goods are produced in a line consisting of six separate stages. A problem at Stage 3 could mean expensive hold-ups at all subsequent stages. However, this problem is minimised if output units from Stage 3 have already been stockpiled ready for processing in Stage 4.

1.7   Another aspect of this example is the question of synchronising Stages 3 and 4. It might ideally be preferable for these two operations to take exactly the same time, so that a smooth flow of output from Stage 3 becomes input to Stage 4, and there is no need for any stockpiling in the middle. However, in practice this might be difficult to achieve. From the production manager's point of view, it might be preferable to produce large batches in Stage 3, leaving Stage 4 staff with plenty of work to be getting on with until a further batch can conveniently be run off in Stage 3.

1.8   All of these examples illustrate the concept of safety stock: the idea that holdings of stock are necessary because unexpected snags are a fact of life and substantial stockholdings enable managers to minimise their worst effects. This whole concept is challenged by modern thinking on just in time production, but it is still undeniably an influence on practising managers.

Service levels

1.9   This notion of safety stock is part of a wider concept of service levels. The point is seen most clearly at the final stage of the production process, where finished goods are made ready for customers. If any problem occurs at this stage there is a risk that service to customers may be damaged. This of course is a serious cause of concern. Anything less than 100 per cent service to customers is regarded as unacceptable.

1.10   Low levels of finished goods stock lead directly to a danger of failing to fulfil customer orders. There is an opportunity cost of losing sales and damaging customer goodwill if demand cannot be met because of **stockouts**. Though it is intangible and hard to measure, most managers would accept that this cost is an extremely important one.

1.11   Extending this concept back through the production process, it is commonly held now that each production department has 'customers' consisting of other departments dependent on the outputs it produces. This means that service levels to 'customers' are important throughout the production process. And in fact it does not stop there: procurement departments also have 'customers', such as the production departments that cannot function without raw materials purchased from external suppliers.

1.12   These ideas of internal departments being customers and suppliers of other internal departments are common in modern management thinking. At present, our focus is on the level of service that must be provided in this customer-supplier relationship. Clearly, a policy of holding stocks at each point where one department is dependent on another can make it simpler to deliver a required level of service. Unexpected snags are less important.

1.13   Firms sometimes try to measure the service levels achieved in relation to stocks. Often this is part of a defined control system in which performance levels are predetermined and managers are appraised in terms of their success in meeting these levels. In the case of stock, different levels of service could be prescribed depending on the likely consequences. For example, if a particular department requires a particular component and a stockout would have serious effects, a service level of 100 per cent might be prescribed; in less critical cases the required service level might be set at, say, 95 per cent.

1.14   These percentages are calculated quite simply as the ratio of satisfied demands to total demands. For example, if a department requires a total of 1,000 components over a period, and finds that 950 are available immediately on demand, then a service level of 95 per cent has been achieved.

Reducing the purchase price of materials

1.15   One further point is worth mentioning in this context. Other things being equal, procurement staff would prefer to order materials in large quantities from suppliers. For one thing, it simplifies administration: an order for 10,000 units is probably as simple to process as an order for 1,000 units, but need not be repeated for ten times as long a period. For another, there is likely to be a financial incentive for large orders: unit purchase prices will fall as a result of supplier discounts.

1.16   This point might be thought to appeal also to the finance function in an organisation. However, the immediate consequence of large orders is large stocks. The 10,000 units will be used up in the end, but it will take some time. In the meantime, there are large stocks lying around unused. These have to be paid for, stored, insured, and managed, incurring costs that will be examined in more detail later. This factor reduces the enthusiasm of finance staff for a policy of large orders. It also deters procurement staff, who know that the assumption of 'other things being equal' is a gross simplification.

1.17   A refinement of the point being made here occurs in the case of commodities whose prices fluctuate. In such a case it may be tempting to take advantage when prices happen to be low by stocking up with bulk purchases. This minimises the need to purchase at other times when prices may be higher.

The immediate costs of stockouts

1.18   The main risk of being out of stock is that, in many types of organisation, operations would not be able to continue without stocks of necessary materials. The effect of this differs depending on the type of organisation and what it is trying to achieve. In all organisations, however, there is likely to be considerable cost attached to being out of stock.

1.19   In a manufacturing company, the risk is that the production line is likely to stop producing. If this were to continue for any length of time, the company would risk gaining a reputation for poor delivery to its own customers. This would be likely to have the effect of driving customers away, which is something that no company would want.

1.20   In terms of cost, large manufacturers have been known to state that a day's lost production would cost $millions. This might be an exaggeration but there would certainly be a heavy cost associated with losing production. This would, of course, include the cost of losing sales to customers but could also include:

- The cost of having to lay workers off on full pay because of the lack of operations continuing (if the company was out of stock for a long time).
- The cost of heating and lighting buildings that would probably need to remain open.

1.21 Public sector organisations would not be able to continue to offer their service if they did not have enough stock of necessary materials and equipment. This would be particularly serious in hospitals because it is possible that certain types of medical care would not be possible until stocks were replenished. Thankfully, this is a rare occurrence.

1.22 In other types of public sector organisation, lack of stock to make emergency repairs could be serious. For example, imagine that one of the water supply companies has a broken water main. If it does not have stock of items to make the repair, there will be flooding in the area and lack of water supply to local residents.

1.23 In the retail sector, if supermarkets lacked stock of some items, it is likely that a customer finding the supermarket to be out of stock and being able to locate the item at a competitor would not return to the first supermarket. In an extremely competitive market this would potentially be quite serious.

2 The costs of acquiring inventories

Costs of ordering stock

2.1 So far we have looked at reasons for holding stocks. There are also good reasons for not holding stocks, or at least for minimising stock levels. One of the most important reasons is that stockholding incurs costs. For certain categories of costs, the higher the level of stock, the higher the level of expenditure.

2.2 However, the equation is not as simple as this might suggest. Paradoxically, some costs actually decrease as stock levels rise. This is because high stock levels are associated with large and infrequent orders, which means that the actual costs of ordering (mainly clerical costs) tend to be lower in environments where stock levels are high.

2.3 In the paragraphs that follow we often refer to the costs of opting for large orders and the costs of holding stock as though they were the same thing. This is because a policy of infrequent large orders leads inevitably to a policy of high stock levels, whereas frequent small orders imply low stock levels.

2.4 There is a trade-off between stockholding costs and stock ordering costs. Careful analysis can identify an **economic order quantity**, being the quantity of an item we should regularly order if we wish to minimise the total costs of ordering and holding stock. We will not pursue this analysis here: our concern is simply to identify what kinds of expenditure arise as a result of ordering and holding stock. We begin with the costs of acquiring stock.

2.5 The costs of acquiring stock include several elements.

- The once-for-all cost of setting up and maintaining an information system for processing orders. For example, an organisation will employ clerical staff, and purchase computer equipment and software to handle ordering and payment procedures.
- The cost of preparing an order requisition each time stock is required.
- The cost of selecting a supplier, perhaps involving the comparison of several different quotations.
- The cost of preparing and processing a purchase order.
- The cost of preparing and processing a goods received note.

- The cost of clerical time, stationery, postage or fax charges incurred each time an order is placed.
- The cost of preparing and processing payment.

2.6 Note also that a policy of frequent small orders can mean loss of supplier discounts that might be available for larger quantities.

2.7 Clearly, most of these costs are reduced if orders are infrequent. However, in that case the orders will be large in volume and stock levels will be high. This is the trade-off already mentioned.

2.8 The above discussion has referred to buying in stock from external suppliers, but there is an equivalent price to pay when goods are manufactured for stock. In this case the costs corresponding to acquisition costs are the set-up costs for the production process. Frequent set-ups to produce small batches each time mean low average stock levels, but higher set-up costs. Infrequent production runs, with large batches each time, mean low set-up costs but high stock levels.

2.9 One final cost associated with frequent orders and low stock levels has already been mentioned. That is the opportunity cost of losing sales and damaging customer goodwill if demand cannot be met because of **stockouts**.

3 The costs of excess inventories

A policy of placing large orders for stock

3.1 To avoid the costs of frequent small orders we might decide instead to opt for infrequent, but larger, orders. This will mean that we often have more stock on hand than we have an immediate use for (ie we will hold excess inventory). This policy also leads to certain costs.

3.2 The most obvious cost in this category is the actual purchase price that must be paid to suppliers. Of course, this must be paid eventually, and you might therefore think that the question of small or large orders is irrelevant. However, that is not the case. There is an **opportunity cost** involved in placing infrequent large orders. What this means is that cash must be paid out sooner in a large lump, instead of gradually in small instalments. In the meantime the business loses the use of cash which might otherwise be put to profitable use elsewhere.

3.3 This concept of opportunity cost is important. It does not refer to cash actually paid out. Instead, it refers to cash that we have an opportunity to earn, but which we forgo because of the decisions we make. In the example we are discussing, by paying for stock sooner rather than later we lose the use of the cash paid out (we lose the opportunity to invest that cash profitably and earn interest or profit).

3.4 A measure of the opportunity cost involved here is easily derived. Take the very simplest assumption: that any spare cash is simply held in a bank deposit account earning interest at a rate of 5 per cent per annum. Now consider a firm's requirement for Component X, which is expected to amount to 120,000 units during the coming year. The purchase price is $2 per unit, and the firm is debating whether to purchase the whole annual requirement now or instead to purchase 10,000 units each month.

3.5 If the whole amount is purchased now, there is an immediate dent in the firm's bank balance to the tune of $240,000. If instead monthly orders are made the $240,000 leaves the bank deposit account steadily at the rate of $20,000 per month. This portion of the firm's bank balance gradually reduces over the year from $240,000 to zero. On average this is equivalent to holding $120,000 in the bank for the whole year. The interest earned at 5 per cent would be $6,000. This is the amount lost if the firm instead decides to place a single order and hold stock over the year: it is the opportunity cost of paying for stock sooner rather than later.

3.6   Other costs also arise from this decision. For example, how are the 120,000 units to be stored? The firm must use storage space, which means paying to build a warehouse or stores area, or possibly renting space. Either way, there is a large storage cost involved. There must also be employees to man the warehouse and to deliver the components to production as required.

3.7   In the meantime, the stock must be insured. The firm cannot afford the risk of serious damage to the warehouse and the stock it contains, so insurance premiums must be included in the cost of stockholding. Even without external factors such as fire or flooding, there may be damage to the stock from natural deterioration or obsolescence.

3.8   It is no easy matter to calculate all of the costs involved here. Even if it were feasible in theory, the procedure would be time-consuming and irksome. In practice, most firms use a rule of thumb method. They express total stockholding costs in terms of a simple percentage. For example, a particular firm may calculate that on average the cost of holding items in stock for a year is about 25 per cent of the purchase price (or production cost) of those items.

3.9   Purchase price and production costs are usually known because they have to be recorded and reviewed for accounting and control reasons, so this assumption gives a simple and quick method of calculation. However, the percentage applied must be supported by careful consideration of the particular circumstances of each organisation, and of the nature of the stock items held.

3.10   One factor in particular is the value of the stock items per cubic metre of storage space. For example, many of the costs involved in storing 20,000 tonnes of cement for a year would be unchanged if the cement were replaced with an equivalent amount of a valuable metal. And yet applying a straight percentage (say 25 per cent) to the value of each would lead to a very different estimate of annual stockholding costs, because the purchase price of the cement is much lower than that of the metal.

3.11   It is convenient to summarise the various categories of cost discussed so far. See Table 6.1 below. We will then go on to discuss some of the holding costs in more detail.

Table 6.1 *Costs of acquiring (producing) stock and holding stock*

COSTS OF ACQUIRING (PRODUCING) STOCK	COSTS OF HOLDING STOCK (EXCESSIVE INVENTORIES)
Setting up and maintaining an information system for processing orders	Opportunity costs of funds tied up in purchase of large orders
Preparing an order requisition	Owning or renting warehouse or stores space
Selecting a supplier	Employing warehouse or stores staff
Preparing and processing a purchase order	Insuring stock
Preparing and processing a goods received note	Deterioration of stock
Clerical time, stationery, postage or fax charges	Obsolescence of stock
Preparing and processing payment	
Loss of bulk purchase discounts	
Production set-up costs	
Opportunity costs of stockouts	

The cost of security

3.12   In some warehouses, this can be a perennial problem. Some warehouses store a great many valuable and 'attractive' items. If they are stolen in significant quantities, the company will lose a large amount of value each year, thus greatly increasing the cost of storage. Other warehouses may not carry such valuable items but may suffer from internal pilferage of such things as small tools.

3.13   As a general rule, if people want to get hold of the items you carry in your warehouse badly enough, they will find a way of doing so. This is particularly true of 'attractive' items. These are usually items that would be useful at home or which could be sold on at a good price. Warehouse managers must do everything possible to keep such theft and pilferage to a minimum.

3.14   Here are some specific measures that may be taken to reduce or eliminate theft and pilferage.

- Limit access so that only stores personnel are allowed to enter the warehouse. This will minimise, if not eliminate, pilferage of stock items.
- Keep buildings locked when not in use and consider employing a watchman or security staff. Remember that outside security companies can provide various levels of service for out-of-hours surveillance. Such a service would incur a cost but this could well be outweighed by reducing or eliminating stock losses.
- All goods received should be checked accurately for quantity, weight, specification etc. Remember that, if you do not know what has arrived, it is unlikely that you will know if items are going missing.
- Adequate systems of stock-checking and auditing should be implemented. These measures keep a constant check on what you have and should inform you of anything going missing. Knowledge of what items are going missing helps you to take steps elsewhere to prevent it.
- Correctly authorised issues – items should only be issued against a properly signed and authorised requisition.
- Adequate records to be maintained – if you do not know what you have and keep a record of what comes in and what goes out, you will not know if anything is going missing.

- Delivery drivers confined to Goods Receiving bay – limiting the number of people allowed access to the warehouse helps to narrow down the list of possible suspects if pilferage does occur.
- Co-operate with Crime Prevention Officer (CPO) on modern security methods etc. The CPO can advise on, for example, weak points of the building, and on modern security systems.
- Designated key-holders for 24-hour issues. If out-of-hours issues are required it is best to ensure that a responsible person, such as the night shift supervisor, takes charge of it.
- Valuable and attractive items should be segregated. It makes sense to keep items deemed particularly prone to theft in a lockable cupboard or cage.
- Staff should be aware that, if they are caught pilfering, the penalty is likely to be instant dismissal and prosecution. This might seem a hard line but a strong message must be sent out, particularly where pilferage is common.
- Scrap and items for disposal should be segregated and kept securely. You should remember that such materials, particularly those that will command a good scrap value, are likely to be attractive.

The cost of insurance

3.15   Stock should be insured against the risks of fire, theft or damage. The value of goods held in stock will have direct bearing on insurance premiums, covering loss or damage, for the warehouse. Insurance premiums usually increase as stock value increases and decrease as stock value decreases.

The use of space

3.16   This brings us to **use of space**. The greater the quantity of stock held, the more space will be required in the stores building. Once again, if we can reduce the amount of stock held to a reasonable minimum, we can reduce the size of the warehouse.

3.17   Thus, use of space is a measure of stores efficiency. If a warehouse is largely empty, the cost of rent and rates, the cost of heating, lighting and power and other costs such as labour and the cost of storage and handling equipment are wasted and are nothing more than a drain on company finances. It is important, therefore, to ensure that the warehouse is as full as it needs to be to provide the organisation's required service level.

3.18   This is not to suggest that the warehouse should be filled simply to achieve this target. If the warehouse is too large, then it is wasting money for reasons just mentioned and thought should be given to 'hiving off' some of it for other purposes or, in extreme cases, renting some of it to outside organisations for temporary storage accommodation.

3.19   If we are in a position to plan a new warehouse building, we should plan it with anticipated demand in mind for as long a period of time into the future as possible. This should ensure that the warehouse is not too large for foreseeable requirements.

Damage to stock

3.20   If items in stock are handled carelessly, they might become damaged. Clearly, this is most likely to be the case with fragile items such as those made of glass. However, even sturdier items such as those made of steel could become bent if dropped. Also, apparently sturdy material such as concrete blocks could become chipped if knocked over.

3.21   Such damage might cause the items to be useless. This means that they would need to be replaced at extra cost to the organisation. In this situation they would need to be 'written off', meaning that the money spent on them was wasted. Additionally, the money spent on the items could not be recovered by selling them to other users. Some of their value might be recovered by selling them for scrap but this, of course, would only recoup a fraction of their original value. Insurance could mitigate this problem.

3.22   The occurrence of damaged stock can be reduced as follows.

- Check stock carefully as it is received into stores. Damaged or inadequate packaging needs action to ensure that the stock will be protected.
- Use stock in the order in which it is received.
- Maintain conditions that are appropriate to the type of stock – for example, in terms of temperature, humidity and so on.
- Train all staff in the use of handling equipment and stress the importance of moving stock items carefully.

Deterioration of stock

3.23   This has a similar effect on the cost of storage but is different in nature. Deterioration happens to some types of items or material if they are kept in stock for a long time. Examples include the following (there are many other possibilities).

- Paper can become discoloured.
- Iron and steel items can become rusty.
- Damp could cause cement to become solid and therefore unusable.

3.24   As with damage, deterioration will increase the cost of storage because it means that items affected will be useless. As with damaged items, items that have deteriorated will incur costs of replacement. Once again, they may be able to be sold for scrap, which would mitigate such costs. Insurance, also, would help mitigate such losses.

3.25   The likelihood of deterioration could be minimised by reducing stockholding. More effective, however, would be to ensure that goods likely to deteriorate are stored in suitable conditions. An example would be keeping materials that are susceptible to damp in dry locations.

The cost of depreciation

3.26   Many items that are held in stock for any length of time will depreciate in value. In other words, their value will diminish because they will be perceived as being 'old'. This would apply particularly to retail items. An example might be where supermarkets sell items that are approaching their 'sell by' date below their normal retail price. Depreciation applies to all stock items, however, and is one reason why it is not considered a good idea to hold larger quantities of stock than are necessary.

Theft and fraud

3.27   These are related in that both refer to illegal activity affecting stocks. Theft is countered with security, as discussed earlier.

3.28   Fraud may arise because a member of staff is seeking to achieve an illicit personal gain. It might also occur where staff are trying to mask inefficiencies such as losses of stock items.

3.29   Here are some typical warehouse frauds arising from criminal activity.

- Claiming that materials have been delivered short by the supplier – when in fact the consignment was delivered fully and correctly.
- Claiming that materials were received as damaged or faulty from the supplier – when in fact the consignment was delivered in good condition.
- Over-picking an order so that surplus materials are on the warehouse floor – ready to be picked up and taken away.
- Putting extra materials on to a delivery vehicle for an unauthorised delivery.
- Plain petty theft.
- Failing to book in certain attractive stock returns (items returned by users or customers because they are not needed) and stealing the materials.

3.30   Fraud carried out to mask losses or inefficiencies might include over-valuing stocks or materials in order to hide losses incurred elsewhere.

3.31   We need to eliminate or, at least, minimise fraud. Documentation for issue should be required for any materials to be issued out of the warehouse area. Issuing materials without the correct documentation will lead to stock losses and create a possibility of fraudulent practices. Nowadays, issuing stocks without any documentation is only likely to occur within very small warehousing functions or privately owned businesses.

3.32   The documents warehouses require to issue out materials may be computer generated and highly detailed with barcodes etc, or may just be a basic record of the quantity that has been issued out and to whom. The key requirement of the documentation is that it creates an 'audit trail'. In other words, if there is a discrepancy between the book stock and the physical stock, documentation is in place to trace where the error has occurred. ('Book stock' means the amount of stock indicated by the company's records; it may differ from 'physical stock', which is the amount of stock actually present.)

3.33   Traditionally signatures are required to issue goods out, but with modern technology individuals may possess barcode identification. If the record is 'swiped' with a 'wand' or 'reader' then you are registered as the stock issuer. Users of stock items or customers may be provided with PIN numbers or passwords to allow them to receive items legitimately.

Obsolescence and redundancy

3.34   **Obsolescence** is usually due to items being held in stock for long periods of time. During this time advancing technology makes the items outdated. In a retail organisation, customers would no longer want to purchase such items. In other types of organisation, it would almost certainly mean that the person(s) who had requested the item would no longer want it.

3.35   Costs lost through obsolescence might be mitigated by selling the item secondhand. A better approach would be to reduce the possibility of it occurring by accurately forecasting usage. Then items could be purchased and held in stock in small quantities and only replenished when those in stock had been used.

3.36   **Redundancy** occurs when items are held in stock for a long time and there comes a point where they are no longer required. Such a situation usually originates from purchasing the item in too large a quantity to start with. In retail organisations, particularly those selling items that are subject to fashion, redundancy might occur because of changes in consumers' tastes.

3.37 Redundant items would need to be sold secondhand or for scrap, once again meaning a loss of value. The best way of mitigating the effects of redundancy would be to forecast requirements as accurately as possible. Again, you could add to this the idea of purchasing the item in small quantities frequently rather than a large quantity at one time. Any loss of bulk discount occurring because of this would probably be outweighed by the fact that the items do not become redundant. It might also be possible, if forecasting can be accurate, to negotiate a discount based on annual consumption whilst scheduling small, frequent, deliveries.

Chapter summary

- One important reason for holding stock is as a safety measure to protect against disruption to production and against failure to meet customer demand.
- A key aspect of inventory management is the need to achieve high service levels. In most cases, a demand for stock items should be satisfied immediately from stock on hand.
- Ordering large quantities of stock has other advantages also, such as the possibility of bulk discounts and the reduced clerical and administrative costs. These benefits must be balanced against the costs of holding large stocks.
- Costs of acquiring stock include the initial cost of setting up a system, and the administrative costs of placing orders.
- Costs of holding stocks include actual cash paid out for items such as warehouse space, insurance, stores staff etc. There is also an opportunity cost (ie a cost measured by the potential income we forfeit by tying up cash in stock).

Self-test questions

Numbers in brackets refer to the paragraphs where you can check your answers.

1   How can holding stock avoid disruption to production in a manufacturing environment? (1.6, 1.7)

2   How is a stock service level calculated? (1.14)

3   Why might finance staff not welcome a policy of large order quantities? (1.16)

4   List some of the costs involved in acquiring stock. (2.5)

5   What is meant by an opportunity cost? (3.2)

6   List measures to reduce theft and pilferage. (3.14)

7   List measures to reduce the occurrence of damaged stock. (3.22)

CHAPTER 7

Techniques for Ordering Inventories

Assessment criteria and indicative content

2.3 Describe techniques commonly used for ordering inventories

- Re-order point control and re-order quantities
- MRP and MRPII systems
- Just in time approaches
- Enterprise resource planning systems

Section headings

1 Dependent and independent demand
2 Stock replenishment systems
3 MRP and MRPII
4 Just in time approaches
5 Enterprise resource planning

1 Dependent and independent demand

Defining dependent and independent demand

1.1 Some stock items are subject to dependent demand, while for other items demand is independent. The distinction is important because different systems of stock control apply to the two categories.

1.2 **Independent demand** is the easier of the two to understand so we will deal with this one first. An item has independent demand characteristics if its demand is **not dependent** on the demand for anything else. The majority of items have independent demand. For example, the demand for desks in an office is not dependent on the demand for anything else. The demand for lubricants in a factory is not dependent on the demand for anything else, and so on. Many consumables and MRO items are subject to independent demand.

1.3 **Dependent demand** is usually encountered in manufacturing organisations. If we take cars as an example, the demand for engines will be dependent on the demand for cars. We can then add that the demand for gear boxes will be dependent on the demand for engines. Demand for the various cogs that go into a gearbox will be dependent on the demand for gearboxes and so on. Ultimately, demand for each component depends upon the demand for the finished product.

1.4 In non-manufacturing environments it is difficult to identify examples of dependent demand. We could, however, say that in a fast food restaurant demand for plastic utensils might be dependent on the demand for takeaway cooked food.

Inventory control systems for dependent demand

1.5 Inventory control (or 'stock control': the terms are interchangeable) is the process of ensuring that we have enough (but not too much) stock of an item. It concerns re-ordering stock when necessary so as to ensure that we continue to have enough stock. It also concerns ensuring that we do not run out of stock (a stockout).

1.6 All the systems that carry out this function involve monitoring stock usage and taking the necessary action to re-order as well as being aware of situations when we have too much stock of an item.

1.7 Stock control systems designed for items of independent demand do not work well with dependent demand items. In fact, it is often said that the failure of these systems to deal with dependent demand items is their main weakness. They also tend to assume that usage of items is smooth and constant. On production lines, however, demand often occurs at different times and in increments of varying size (a phenomenon known as 'lumpy' demand).

1.8 In the next section we look at stock replenishment systems for independent demand items. In the section after that we look at systems designed for dependent demand: MRP and MRPII.

2 Stock replenishment systems

2.1 The aim of stock management, for independent demand items, is to set up a regular system for monitoring levels of stock, and planning to replenish them in time to meet forecast demand (the right quantity at the right time) – while generally carrying as little stock as possible. There are two main methods for doing this.

- Periodic review systems, in which the stock level of an item is reviewed at regular or fixed intervals, and, depending on the quantity in stock, a replenishment order is placed for whatever quantity appears to be appropriate.
- Fixed order point systems, in which stock of an item is replenished with a predetermined quantity when inventory falls to a predetermined re-order level (ROL) or fixed order point

2.2 Let's look at each of these approaches in turn.

Periodic review

2.3 In periodic review systems (also called fixed interval ordering, scheduling systems or 'topping up' systems), the stock level of the product is examined on a periodic (fixed time interval) basis, and, depending on the quantity in stock, a replenishment order is placed to 'top up' stock to the desired level. In other words, the order quantity is not fixed, but the timing of orders is. Replenishment quantities vary, being whatever is sufficient to bring stock levels up to a predetermined stock level – or whatever is needed to last through the next interval, or until the next delivery. This can be depicted as follows: Figure 7.1.

Figure 7.1 *Periodic review system*

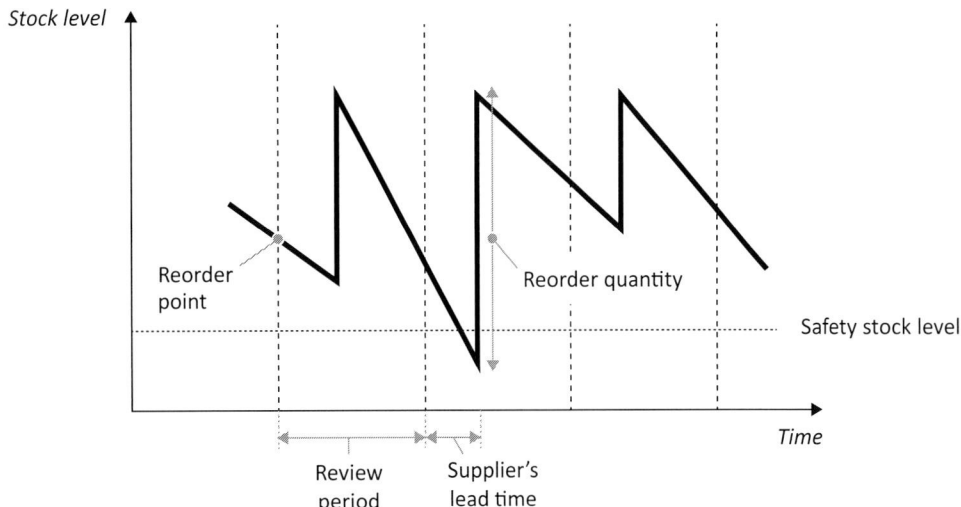

2.4   The length of the review period will be determined on an item-by-item (or category-by-category) basis, depending on usage patterns. The shorter the review period, the more effort and cost is involved, so it is usual to apply an ABC analysis: Category A items might be reviewed weekly, Category B items monthly and Category C items quarterly, say.

2.5   The review itself can be undertaken by periodic physical inspection by stores staff ('stocktake'), or by a computerised or manual system that records ongoing purchases, requisitions and returns of each item to give a running total of stock held at any given time. (This latter system is sometimes called **perpetual inventory**, because it is carried out on a constant basis.)

2.6   Computerised systems often use barcode scanning to input stock data to the system. A more modern alternative is **radio frequency identification** (RFID): an electronic tagging system which does not require item-by-item scanning to input stock data, but simply 'reads' the signals given out by electronic tags on stock.

2.7   Once the current stock level has been established at a given review point, the decision must be taken on how much to order to replenish the stock to a desired level. Take a monthly review system, for example. At the 1st January review point, an order will be made based on the quantities of the item likely to be required during January; *plus* enough stock to cover the lead time for delivery following a review and order on the 1st February; *plus* an appropriate level of safety stock.

2.8   In other words, the size of the order will be calculated as: forecast demand over the forthcoming review interval; *plus* forecast demand over the lead time for replenishment (ordering and delivery) in the following review interval; *plus* safety or buffer stock; minus current stock levels; minus stock already on order but not yet delivered.

2.9   The *advantages* and *disadvantages* of a periodic review or fixed interval ordering system are listed in Table 7.1.

Table 7.1 *Advantages and disadvantages of periodic review systems*

ADVANTAGES	DISADVANTAGES
Ease of administration and control, with predictable workload planning for procurement and warehousing staff (at fixed review or replenishment periods)	The risk of unexpected stockouts, since the system assumes that there will be no review of stock other than at the fixed interval. This necessitates the use of safety stocks.
Orders may be placed at the same time for a number of items, enabling the consolidation of shipments, reduced transport costs, or quantity discounts from suppliers	Higher average stocks than with fixed order point systems, because of the need to provide for review periods, lead times and safety stocks
Ability to identify slow-moving or obsolete stock items, due to periodic stock review.	Re-order quantities not based on economic order quantities
	Waste of time reviewing stock levels which do not require action.

Fixed order point and re-order level (ROL)

2.10 In a fixed order point (or re-order point) system, stock of an item is replenished with a predetermined (fixed order) quantity when inventory falls to a predetermined minimum level (the re-order level or ROL). In other words – directly opposite to the periodic review approach – the timing of the order isn't fixed, but the quantity is. The system is illustrated in Figure 7.2.

Figure 7.2 *Fixed order point systems*

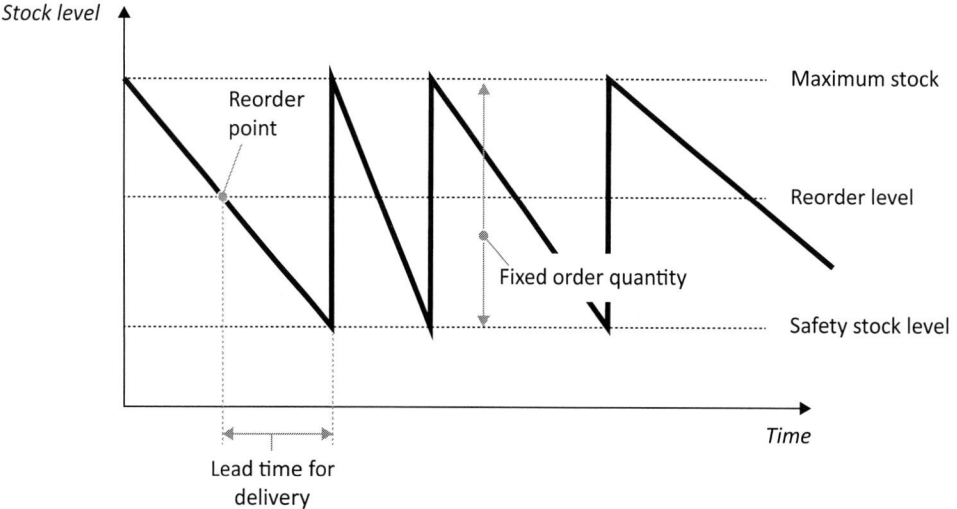

2.11 To determine the re-order point for a particular item, managers rely on past experience of demand and usage patterns for the item, taking into account any known factors which may lessen or increase demand or usage in the coming period. The aim is to fix on a stock level sufficient to keep the business in stock during the supplier's delivery lead time, plus a reserve of safety stock. In other words, a basic re-order level (ROL) should be equal to:

- Maximum amount used × maximum lead time for replenishment; *or*
- (Average amount used × average lead time) + safety stock

2.12 Once stock falls to this predetermined order point or ROL, the system triggers a replenishment order.

- A common manual method for doing this is a two-bin system. We keep a stock item in two bins. We withdraw stock from one bin for use in production until the bin is empty. At that point we place an order for new stock. While we are waiting for this to arrive we use the stock from the second bin.
- Computerised perpetual inventory systems (using barcoding or RFID to record inputs and withdrawals of stock and maintain running totals) may be used to automatically trigger replenishment orders when inventory has fallen to the specified re-order point.

2.13 In either case, the re-order quantity is the same each time. For items of high value, it may be sensible to use a structured approach to determining what this quantity should be, perhaps by using the economic order quantity (a quantity calculated so as to minimise the total of acquisition costs and holding costs). For small-value items, simple decision rules (based on usage rates) may be more cost-effective.

2.14 Advantages and disadvantages of a fixed order quantity or ROL system are summarised in Table 7.2.

Table 7.2 *Advantages and disadvantages of fixed order point systems*

ADVANTAGES	DISADVANTAGES
Ability to use the economic order quantity, unlike periodic review systems	Acceptance of the holding cost (which may be expensive if the stock levels are set too high)
Lower average levels of stock than with periodic review systems, because of enhanced responsiveness to demand fluctuations	Assumption that stock usage patterns and lead times are predictable and stable. Parameters must be reviewed, to avoid risk of stockouts (if demand is higher, or lead time longer, than foreseen) – or excess stock (eg if replenished in full, despite fall-off of demand).
Automatic 'triggering' of replenishment by the system, without time being wasted on items where the stock level is satisfactory.	Inefficiencies, from inappropriate order points and quantities and/or from ordering of individual items at different times. Eg: frequent uneconomical small orders.
	Risk of overloading procurement systems and staff, if multiple items reach their re-order levels at the same time.

3   MRP and MRPII

3.1 Before we consider how to control inventory of dependent demand items, we need to look at the nature of production lines. The first concept to consider is the **hierarchy of components**. If you do not have experience of working in a manufacturing environment you may find this concept rather difficult to grasp. The example shown below (Figure 7.3), based on car production, should help.

Figure 7.3 *The hierarchy of components in car manufacture*

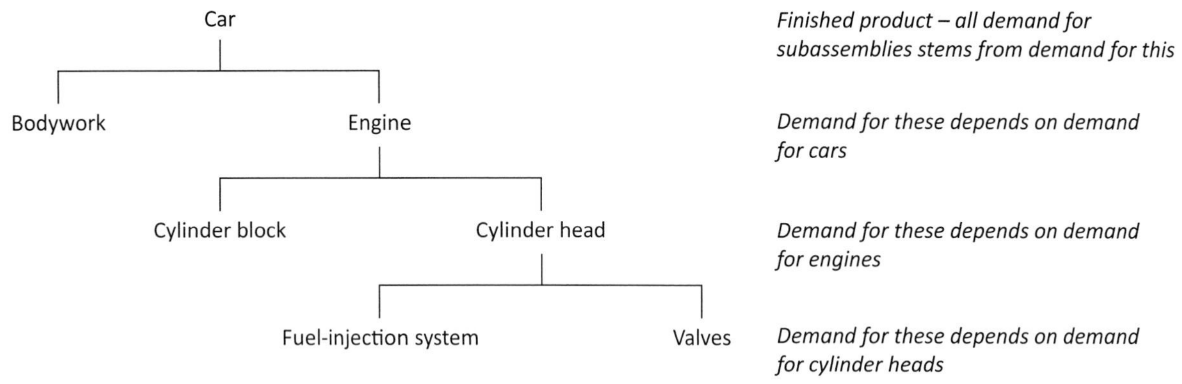

Car	*Finished product – all demand for subassemblies stems from demand for this*
Bodywork / Engine	*Demand for these depends on demand for cars*
Cylinder block / Cylinder head	*Demand for these depends on demand for engines*
Fuel-injection system / Valves	*Demand for these depends on demand for cylinder heads*

Materials requirements planning

3.2 The next problem is how to control inventory of dependent demand items if traditional systems do not really work. In recent decades much work has been done in developing more sophisticated systems to cope with this situation. The most commonly used system is materials requirements planning (MRP). This is invariably an IT-based system that helps determine when items are required for a production line and in what quantities. It can operate manually but this is very rare and would really only work for finished goods containing few components.

3.3 MRP is based on a **master production schedule (MPS)**. This is derived from the company's sales forecast, updated with the latest actual sales information. This provides an estimate of orders that will need to be satisfied during the time period under consideration. Typically, this period would be the next 12 months for a 'mass production' company (a car manufacturer being a good example).

3.4 To the sales forecast would be added actual customer orders, and the company's production policy would also be taken into consideration. The production policy covers matters such as whether the company produces on a 'batch' basis or is a 'jobbing' concern. It would also cover such aspects as whether we will produce Product A (for example) for the next two months or whether it will be Product B and so on. It is likely that a 'batch' producer would have a policy of producing one product for, say, the next month. It would then change its production process to produce another of its product range for, say, two months.

3.5 To give an example of this, consider a hypothetical manufacturer of forklift trucks with two production lines. In Month 1, the first production line is devoted to producing 1,000kg capacity electric pallet trucks, while the second production line is producing 2,000kg capacity diesel forklift trucks. The tooling and equipment is then changed on both lines. During Month 2, the first line produces 1,500kg capacity 'rider' pallet trucks while the second line produces 1,000 kg capacity 'reach' trucks. The types of truck produced, the quantities and the timings would all be dictated by customer orders.

3.6 Once the MPS has been produced, the next stage is to 'explode' it. This means that the computer software calculates how many of each component is required in order to manufacture the finished products specified in the MPS. The document that results from this process is known as a **bill of materials** (BOM).

3.7 We can illustrate this by reference to our fictional forklift manufacturer. Suppose the MPS shows that 200 1,000kg capacity trucks are to be produced. The BOM will show that 800 wheels are required (four per truck), meaning 4,000 wheel nuts (five per wheel) and so on. The BOM will follow this process for every component and subassembly in the entire truck. This is illustrated in Figure 7.4.

Figure 7.4 *Exploding the MPS into the BOM*

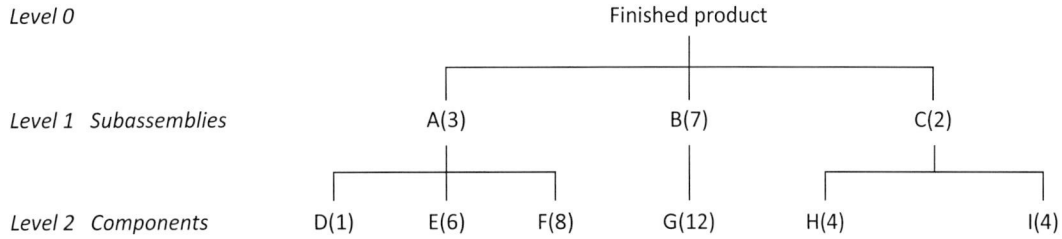

3.8 The MPS and BOM can be converted into an MRP system by adding the following information into the system's database.

- The inventory status file: this tells us which of the required items we already have in stock and in what quantities
- The delivery lead times for all of the items required
- All of these pieces of information should tell us **what** we need to order, in what **quantities** and **when** we need to place the orders. This should then ensure that the right quantities of the right items are delivered to us not too long before being required by the production line.
- With items being used regularly, it is not uncommon to place them on call-off orders or to use consignment stocking. This is particularly true of items with short lead times and which are readily available.

3.9 In summary, the MRP process is as follows.

- Obtain updated sales forecast – updated with latest *actual* sales information.
- Use sales forecast, customer orders and production policy to form master production schedule. (MPS)
- Use MRP software to compute material requirements by 'exploding' end product requirements into successively lower levels in the product structure. This gives the gross requirement for each material and component.
- Use the inventory status file to determine materials and components already in stock. Deduct this from the **gross requirement** to arrive at the **net requirement** for each material and component (ie the quantities we need to order from suppliers).
- Assess the net requirement in the light of supplier lead times in order to determine the schedule for ordering materials and components.
- Place orders with suppliers via the procurement function
- Receive goods and issue them to the production line.

3.10 This is illustrated in Figure 7.5.

Figure 7.5 *The MRP process*

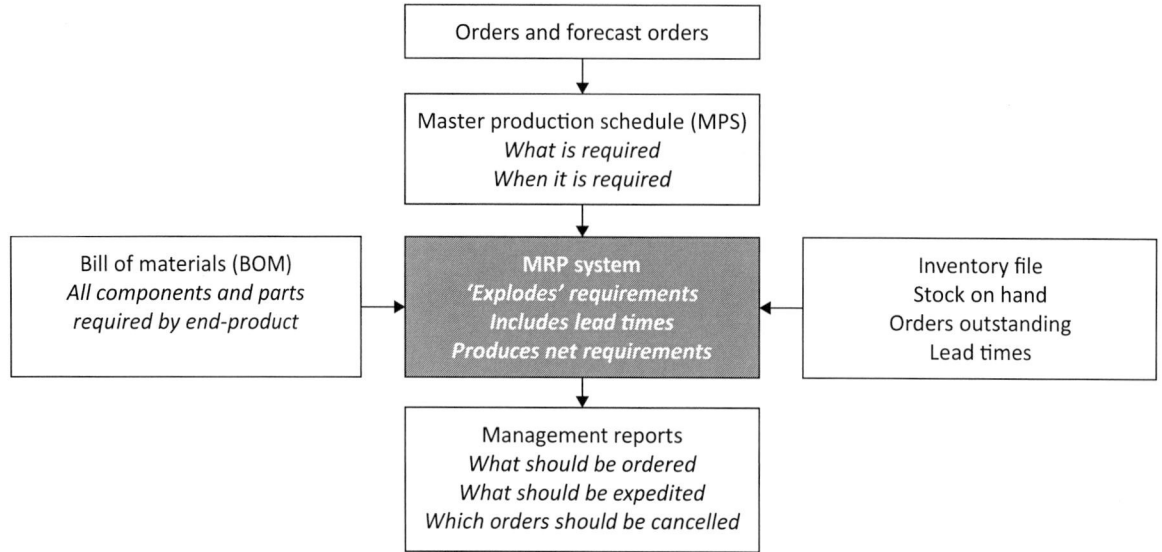

Characteristics of MRP

3.11 There are certain **prerequisites** for using MRP.

- There must be a master production schedule exploded into a bill of materials.
- All inventory items must be identified.
- The bill of materials must exist at planning stage.
- The inventory status of all items is needed.
- File data must have integrity.
- Lead times for each material and component must be known and updated on an ongoing basis.
- All of the quantity relationships to end products must be known (eg how many wheels to a truck; how many wheel nuts to a wheel, etc).
- There must be reliable, flexible suppliers who are committed to supplying against MRP schedules and who will make the system work.

3.12 The advantages of MRP are as follows.

- It reduces inventory.
- It is sensitive to change. Data can be updated as frequently as is necessary.
- It provides a look into the future by forecasting what products are to be produced and what materials will be needed to produce them.
- Order quantities are related to actual requirements. This is one of the main reasons why MRP reduces inventory.
- MRP reduces 'routine time' in the procurement job. This is particularly true if requirements are known for a relatively long period of time and remain steady during that time.
- It integrates the thinking and action of personnel in Procurement, Production and Marketing. This is because it requires information from all three departments as we have seen above.

3.13 The limitations (not necessarily disadvantages) of MRP are as follows.

- It only applies to 'dependent' demand items.
- Its payback on low-value items (Category C items: see earlier in this chapter) may be doubtful. This is because it might be advantageous just to keep fairly large quantities of these items in

stock. This would mean that the items would be available when required without costing too much to hold in stock. This in turn would mean that they would also only need to be ordered infrequently, so that the cost of ordering would be low.

- It depends on an accurate forecast which is not always possible.
- It does not apply to many 'jobbing' manufacturers who must keep raw materials on hand to meet what amounts to emergency production orders.

3.14   In conclusion, you should be aware that some organisations may face a number of different types of demand at the same time and may, therefore, need to use a combination of systems to cope with this situation. For example, in a car production plant, production line requirements will exhibit dependent demand characteristics and will be catered for by an MRP system (or similar). The plant's maintenance items will exhibit independent demand characteristics and will be catered for by fixed order point or periodic review systems.

Manufacturing resources planning (MRPII)

3.15   The disciplined approach introduced by MRP has been further developed over the years. Manufacturing resources planning (MRPII) builds on key areas of MRP by considering all the resources needed for production, not just materials. For example, it deals with manpower, machinery and money.

3.16   The differences are made clear in their respective names. Materials requirements planning concentrates on securing the right materials to enable the production run to go ahead. Manufacturing resources planning examines the manufacturing resources required for the production to go ahead, eg the labour costs involved, the costs of machinery and proportion of overheads attributable etc. MRPII enables materials and work to be costed accurately.

3.17   MRPII is a method for planning manufacture and assessing the costs involved. It draws on the aggregate plans via the MPS not only to develop the areas covered by an MRP system but also to allow for such areas as personnel deployment, maintenance planning, and financial analysis.

3.18   Building on the discipline required for traditional MRP systems the MRPII model has led some to say that MRPII adds the financial function to MRP.

3.19   Managers can determine the dates when suppliers must be paid by studying MRP timing of purchase orders and their due dates. Accurate costing of manufacturing can be obtained as the system can look at machines and personnel used and analyse the information to provide accurate costings on production runs. The analysis can be further used as a benchmark for future production runs in order to seek operational improvements.

3.20   MRPII is often described as a closed-loop system, in that there is an automatic feedback from the manufacturing function to the MPS, leading to changes in the MPS. This in turn leads to adjustments in manufacturing plans, thus closing the information loop as illustrated in Figure 7.6.

Figure 7.6 *A closed-loop MRPII system*

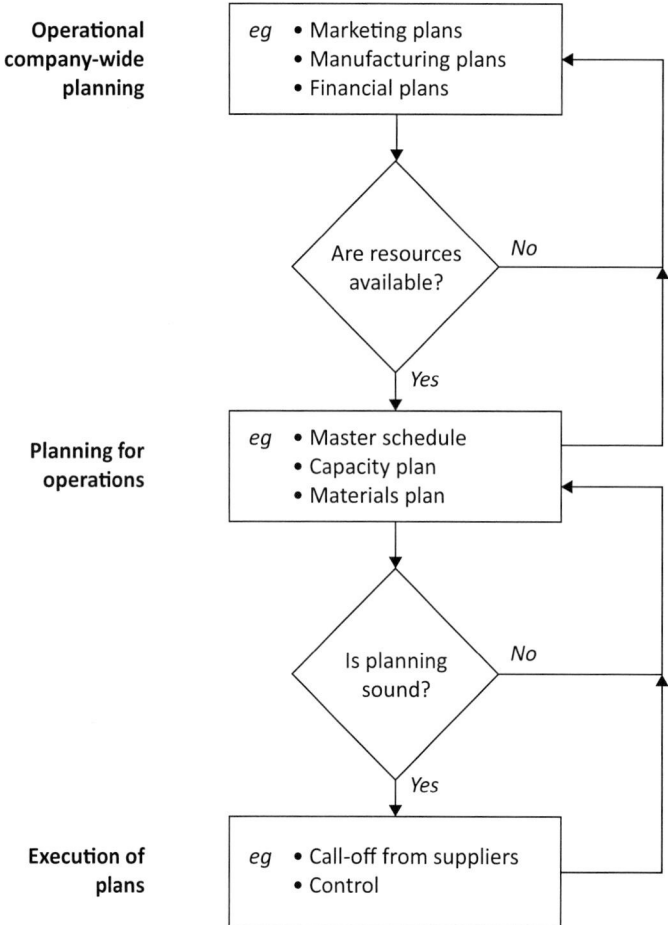

3.21 Closing the loop involves comparing production plans against the availability of resources. MRP makes the assumption that resources required are available. Closed loop MRPII checks whether the required resources are available. If this is not the case then the MPS is modified.

3.22 MRP and MRPII systems have proven themselves particularly in batch manufacture. Although they require ongoing investment in people and system development the rewards in increased professionalism as the system integrates into the organisation can be impressive.

3.23 Manufacturing on a larger scale brings a new range of issues that go beyond the design of MRP and MRPII systems. Just in time (JIT) systems can utilise MRP and MRPII, but MRP shows to best advantage in batch production systems where the need is to schedule production around customer demand and supplier lead times.

4   Just in time approaches

Eliminating waste

4.1 The concept of just in time (JIT) is concerned with the reduction and ultimately the elimination of waste. It is often linked to the concept of **lean supply** – 'lean' meaning more efficient and less wasteful.

4.2 Taiichi Ohno, a Toyota engineer, developed a list of **seven wastes** under the heading of lean supply. The waste that most concerns us is that caused by unnecessary stockholding.

Kanban

4.3   This simply means 'communication' and is the physical means of transmitting requirements to suppliers. It can be achieved electronically, by telephone or fax, or by any other means deemed suitable by both parties. Alternatively, it can simply tell the warehouse manager or personnel that an item needs re-ordering. It could do this by giving an electronic signal when a despatch is made that takes the item's stock to below where it should be. Upon receipt of the signal an order for replenishment of the stock item would be placed with the supplier.

4.4   The **two-bin system** (which we described briefly earlier in this chapter) is a much older, more traditional version of *kanban*. The two-bin approach is probably the simplest form of stock control and stock replenishment, and it operates purely visually. Each item is physically stored in two bins. When the first bin is empty this is a signal that replenishment is required and an order is placed with the supplier. While the order is arriving, the second bin is used. The only possible pitfall with this system is that storekeepers need to be trained only to take items from the first bin until it is empty – if they take items from both bins at the same time, problems could result.

4.5   There are two variations on the theme.

- Both bins are of the same size and hold the same amount of items. When the first bin is empty, re-ordering takes place. When the second bin is empty, this again triggers the ordering process and items from the first bin are used until it in turn is empty. In other words, this is a kind of 'revolving' process.
- The second bin is tailored to hold the amount of stock required in order to see the company through the supplier's lead-time period so that the goods should arrive at about the same time as the second bin becomes empty. In this variation, which could be seen as a slightly more refined version, the first bin is the 'main' one with the second being seen as buffer stock. The order quantity must be sufficient to replenish both bins.

4.6   Waste (especially in terms of excess production) is hugely expensive. The more accurate the demand forecast, the greater the profitability. If demand is not forecast accurately then the result is customer dissatisfaction. Manufacturing companies that are working towards JIT increasingly require deliveries to be made from suppliers direct to the production area.

4.7   This demand-led manufacturing is known as a **pull system**: goods are pulled into stock only when they are needed. The manufacturer aims to produce goods only against known customer orders. With this system there is greater certainty; deliveries, storage and movement to the production line can be accurately planned. JIT is also common in the retail sector, particularly in large supermarket operations. Overall, JIT can be described as a system whereby stocks are pulled through the supply chain by customers.

4.8   In a pull system, storage is integrated by using the *kanban* system. This can be described as 'ordering a box, when one is left on the line'. This two-bin approach replaces the used item with another when the first item has been used. With more general items a minimum quantity (eg 30 items) is held in a tote box. When the 30 units have been used the second box comes forward. The original box is then replenished.

Responsive suppliers

4.9   The JIT concept is a move towards reducing supplier lead times, buyer stockholdings and work in progress. It is based on a positive inventory management policy and needs close co-operation from suppliers to be successful. Whilst the ultimate objective is zero stockholding for the buyer, it is clear that optimum performance could be difficult to achieve unless the supplier holds stocks of the required components. However, reduced delivery times of acceptable specified quality items, as in the MRP system, would result in reduced stockholdings and investment.

4.10 Making this concept work satisfactorily requires reliable and responsive suppliers. This means that, when selecting a supplier, thorough evaluation is essential. This may lead if necessary to **supplier development**: a positive policy of the buying company in extending practical support and assistance to the supplier. It is often said that JIT can be achieved by developing a very close and ongoing relationship with suppliers, supported by the linking of relevant IT systems enabling suppliers to see the customers' production schedules and rate of manufacture and to tailor their production accordingly.

4.11 The facility provided by the supplier in holding stock for JIT delivery would no doubt result in an increased component price, but this would be offset by the reduction of stockholding costs at the buyer's company and the assurance of on-time delivery.

4.12 In JIT systems the demand information comes directly from the purchasing organisation to the supplying organisation. JIT is not a programme for suppliers only, but will only effectively work if the buyer and supplier work as a partnership. Because it requires absolute minimum stocks and reliance, normally, on a sole supplier per type of goods, the information relative to, say, daily requirements has to be notified as accurately and as soon as possible to the supplier. This may mean that the situation is relayed electronically.

4.13 In order to meet frequent orders, the supplier needs the purchaser to forecast demands in advance and notify actual demands as soon as is practical, especially if they deviate significantly from those forecast. Demand information then has to be given within the supplies organisation, to ensure the right quantity of materials is available and is despatched to arrive according to the scheduled requirements.

4.14 The purchasing organisation also has to ensure that it is able to manage and identify what it actually does require and when it requires it. This demands that the organisation has a system for identifying material usage, which is its commitment to the suppliers. The system works because the demand for producing a unit pulls work through. This can be an operation-by-operation pull in the purchasing organisation. If there is no pull, then there is no requirement for the goods.

4.15 JIT requires that the organisation realises what to produce, and the time taken in each phase of production. JIT systems provide the best current application of stock control systems but rely heavily on management commitment and technology to make the operation work. Stock is delivered 'just in time' for manufacture.

4.16 Clearly a JIT system means that there is little margin for error. The product quality must be high and 'fit for purpose' as there is no margin for goods being rejected or reworked. This is a concept known as **zero defects**. Delivery must be on time, every time and in consequence, many suppliers are situated geographically close to their customers.

4.17 In order to be able to achieve JIT much emphasis is placed on having suppliers of the highest possible standard in all aspects of their performance. For this reason, it might be useful for manufacturing companies that are employing JIT to involve suppliers of components and materials at the design and development stage of their product. This might involve sharing commercially sensitive information. This is another reason why supplier evaluation and the development of close supplier relationships would be important.

4.18 In the retail sector, organisations using JIT would need to share sales forecast information and usage figures to enable suppliers to schedule deliveries efficiently.

JIT and MRP

4.19 JIT and MRP can be used together. The MPS forecasts projected total demand for the manufacturing company's product but individual components are 'pulled' through the system, on a JIT basis, as they are required.

4.20 A variation on the JIT theme is **late customisation**. This refers to a manufacturing process where the final processes ('finishing touches') of a product's manufacture are delayed until the customer's exact requirements are known. The example invariably quoted in the literature is that of Dell Computers. A customer ordering a Dell computer provides details of his requirements online. Most of the components required for a computer have already been produced and assembled. Dell then completes the manufacture of the computer in line with the specific order requirements and despatches it to the customer.

4.21 To make such a system work, the manufacturer (Dell is only an example – there are others) must have JIT supplies from its suppliers. If not, it would not be able to produce in line with customer requirements and despatch its finished product to customers, all with very little notice. In such situations, it is the JIT concept and the use of efficient, reliable, suppliers that enable it to work.

Advantages and disadvantages of JIT

4.22 The advantages and disadvantages of JIT are summarised in Table 7.3. We should note that in general, the disadvantages are considered to be outweighed by the potential advantages and cost savings.

Table 7.3 *Advantages and disadvantages of JIT*

ADVANTAGES	DISADVANTAGES
Reducing wastes, maximising added value and minimising costs	Vulnerability to supplier or system failure: no time or stock buffers
Flexibility to meet variable demands and contingencies, through the development of swift response	Potential reduction in production capacity utilisation (traded off with flexibility, customer satisfaction)
Reduced stock levels and lead times, higher quality (required to maintain speed of delivery to customer) and therefore better customer service	Higher price charged by suppliers for delivering on a JIT basis, plus possibly loss of bulk discounts (due to smaller orders).
Employee involvement and empowerment, potentially leading to commitment and proactive improvements	Smaller, more frequent orders (if not organised on the basis of 'call-off' contracts), resulting in higher order costs.
Improved supply chain relationships, and integrated systems	Additional costs of monitoring and managing supplier performance, reliability and quality

4.23 JIT is not appropriate for every organisation, or in all circumstances. There may be problems for a company seeking to operate JIT direct with an overseas supplier, for example, due to:

- Difficulty of developing close collaboration and trust with suppliers, given limited opportunities for communication and interaction
- Difficulties and costs of monitoring supplier performance and quality, given the distance to the supply market (particularly in countries where quality standards are generally lower or less regulated)
- Long delivery lead times, due to the distance goods have to be transported
- Loss of efficiency of transport capacity utilisation, delivering more frequent, smaller consignments
- Increased risk of supply disruption, due to transport risk, environmental risks in the foreign supply market and so on.

4.24 Potential disadvantages of JIT can be summarised as follows.

- It might be necessary to pay a higher unit price for items to suppliers to compensate for the supplier's costs in supplying on a JIT basis. This should be outweighed, however, by the greatly reduced cost of storage that should arise from the use of JIT.
- Following from that, the buyer might lose bulk discounts from suppliers because of small quantities being delivered at any one time. This should not be the case, however, if the buyer is able to forecast total requirements with reasonable accuracy.
- There is great reliance placed on suppliers who must be able to deliver in the ways mentioned above (in terms of quality, time, etc). This is not a disadvantage in itself although, if suppliers let the buyer down, there would be significant problems of lost or delayed production. This is probably the biggest potential disadvantage of JIT.
- Further to this last issue, there might be a cost associated with the evaluation and monitoring of suppliers to ensure their reliability. Again, however, this should be more than outweighed by the advantages that arise from JIT.

5 Enterprise resource planning

Management information systems (MIS)

5.1 Management information is data collected (often from the transaction processing systems of the organisation), processed and formatted in such a way as to be useful to managers to aid them in planning, control and decision-making. Management information tools include the following.

- **Databases and database management systems**: capturing and storing data (eg on customers, products and inventory, suppliers or transactions in progress) in a structured way, so that they can be shared by different users, and interrogated flexibly for a variety of applications.
- **Decision support systems**: eg spreadsheets and computer models, used to examine the effect of different inputs and scenarios on the outcomes of a plan or decision. Examples in procurement include trend and spend analysis tools, and tender evaluation tools.
- **Management information systems**: integrated systems for recording, storing and analysing a wide range of sales, purchase, point-of-sale, inventory, maintenance, HR, financial and business intelligence data, to support management decision-making.

5.2 A key problem in many organisations is that management information is fragmented within the business: separate functional IT systems may have evolved over many years, resulting in 'islands of information', so that information is available to one function but not visible or accessible to other internal (or external) stakeholders. Below we look at modern systems that attempt to overcome this problem.

Enterprise resource planning

5.3   Enterprise resource planning (ERP) is a development of MRP in the direction of further integration. ERP systems consolidate materials, manufacturing, logistics, supply chain, sales and marketing, finance and HR planning information into a single integrated management system: a single database able to offer 'real-time' information for solving a range of business problems.

5.4   CIPS defines ERP as: 'Computer-based systems designed to process an organisation's transactions and facilitate integrated and real-time planning, production and customer response.'

5.5   ERP systems are cross-functional and enterprise-wide. All functions involved in operations are integrated in one system – including manufacturing, warehousing and distribution, accounting, HR, marketing, strategic management and procurement. ERP systems align closely with the concept of supply chain management, and ERPII software extends the system to include links with suppliers and other supply chain stakeholders.

5.6   The benefits claimed for ERP include: integration and automation of many business processes; a general reduction in process costs; efficiency and flexibility gains; standardisation and sharing of data and practices across the enterprise; generating and accessing decision support information on a 'real-time' basis; quicker response times and improved customer service; improved communication and data-sharing; and potentially improved supply chain management and relationships.

Implementing ERP

5.7   An ERP system represents a very large IT investment and commitment: one that requires careful thought and evaluation. Implementation is frequently phased in over a period of anywhere from three months to two years. Software packages offered by the leading suppliers – such as PeopleSoft, SAP, JD Edwards and Oracle – offer this facility, allowing for the adaption of existing, 'legacy' systems (designed to meet the particular needs of different functions).

5.8   Many large companies have successfully integrated ERP systems. Others have not been so successful: Hershey Foods, for example, suffered disruptive distribution problems following a flawed implementation. Further development may be required before ERP technology is genuinely accessible to smaller organisations.

5.9   ERP involves consolidating an enterprise's planning, manufacturing, logistics, supply chain, sales and marketing efforts into one management system.

5.10   To integrate systems across an organisation is a tall order. Each department has its own system designed to meet its particular needs (known as 'legacy' systems). ERP combines them together to form a single, integrated software program that operates off a single database enabling the sharing of information and enhanced communication.

5.11   ERP systems are increasingly being used, at this stage primarily by multinational organisations, to integrate all aspects of the business into one unified database that interfaces across the entire organisation.

5.12   ERP helps the communication between all aspects of a business including human resources, financial accounting, manufacturing, supply-chain management, logistics and sales.

5.13 ERP systems are a development of the MRP approach that enables an examination of the consequences that changes will bring. The same principle forms the basis of ERP systems but on a far wider scale.

5.14 ERP (despite the name) is not a planning system but is more about resources and enterprise. It can have a defined purpose (particularly with supply chain management and financial accounting where resources can be more finely monitored and discrepancies become more apparent), but its main purpose is about gaining competitive advantage for the enterprise as a whole.

5.15 When implementing ERP, an organisation must go through a careful period of strategic planning that will involve a strong and ongoing commitment from senior management. Implementation will take from three months to two years and will prove a costly operation. Existing systems (legacy systems) must be integrated into the new software, and packages and features required from the new system will require development.

5.16 ERP systems provide a generic business model for an organisation to follow. This may cause problems, as most businesses will not fit neatly into this model. It may prove necessary to reconfigure or re-engineer aspects of the business. Software can be customised to meet requirements but at a price.

5.17 Clearly the strategic considerations and possible implementation pitfalls of ERP systems require detailed thought. Here are some relevant considerations.

- Who are our stakeholders?
- Which processes are most important now and why?
- Does the system meet our needs or go beyond them?
- Do we integrate over stages and if we do what sequence should we use?
- Who will be responsible for change management?
- Who will be our change champions?
- What is our business culture and what are its strengths?
- How can we maximise those strengths?
- What are our weak areas and how will we address issues caused by them?
- What will be the toughest changes and how will we address them?

Chapter summary

- Some stock items are subject to independent demand: usage does not depend on demand for anything else. Items are subject to dependent demand if usage depends on the quantity demanded of something else.
- Stock control and replenishment involve ensuring that we have enough stock (without overstocking), as well as triggering the ordering process for new deliveries when we realise that we are running out of stock.
- If demand and/or usage of items is steady and predictable, stock control is relatively straightforward.
- In a periodic review system, the stock level of an item is examined on a periodic (fixed time interval) basis and a replenishment order is placed to top up stock to the desired level.
- In a fixed order quantity system, stock is replenished with a predetermined (fixed order) quantity when inventory falls to the predetermined reorder level.
- To control inventory of dependent demand items we use techniques such as MRP and MRPII. Both are based on producing a master production schedule which is then 'exploded' to produce a bill of materials.
- Just in time procurement and supply is concerned with reducing and eventually eliminating waste in the supply chain.
- *Kanban* systems are a method of achieving just in time supply. Their success depends on finding responsive suppliers who can supply the right quality of materials promptly.
- Enterprise resource planning systems are designed to integrate all the business systems throughout an organisation. They are found mostly in large multinationals.

Self-test questions

Numbers in brackets refer to the paragraphs where you can check your answers.

1 Distinguish between dependent and independent demand. (1.2, 1.3)

2 What are the main purposes of stock control and replenishment? (1.5, 2.1)

3 Distinguish between periodic review systems and fixed order quantity systems. (2.1)

4 List advantages and disadvantages of (a) periodic review systems and (b) fixed order quantity systems. (Table 7.1, Table 7.2)

5 How is a master production schedule produced? (3.3)

6 How is a bill of materials produced from a master production schedule? (3.6)

7 List advantages of MRP. (3.12)

8 Distinguish between MRP and MRPII. (3.15–3.16)

9   Explain how a two-bin system of stock control works. (4.4)

10   List advantages and disadvantages of JIT. (Table 7.3)

11   What is an ERP system? (5.3)

CHAPTER 8

Expediting Supplies

Assessment criteria and indicative content

 Define the processes that should be used when expediting supplies

- Defining expediting
- Problem solving
- Tracking the relevant documentation
- Obtaining written confirmations
- Review agreements made

Section headings

1 Defining expediting
2 Problem solving
3 Tracking the relevant documentation
4 Review agreements made

1   Defining expediting

Expediting orders

1.1 'Expediting' simply means 'assisting the progress' of something. If the buyer has any concerns about delivery (because the supplier is less than reliable, or because on-time delivery is critical), the order may require expediting.

1.2 Expediting may be as simple as a buyer making a phone call to the supplier to check on progress – and it may be natural for the buyer to be responsible for managing timing and delivery, if he has been dealing closely with the supplier on an order. However, a team of full-time expediters may be employed to manage the timing of supply (especially for a complex project, for example). They may be attached to the buying department, or project planning or a user department (which has a strong grasp of schedules and priorities).

1.3 The term 'progress chasing' or 'order chasing' is sometimes used instead of 'expediting': usually meaning an enquiry into how progress is going, or (more often) where an order is when it is late. However, this is a reactive or 'fire fighting' approach, focused on problem solving rather than problem avoidance. Expediting should ideally be a proactive role, as an ongoing part of **contract management**: taking planned steps to ensure that suppliers are able and on schedule to deliver as agreed in the supply contract.

1.4 Not all orders will be worth the effort and cost of expediting, so the first requirement will be to prioritise deliveries, identifying those for which:

- There is a higher risk of delivery problems (because the supplier is unknown to the buyer, or has a poor or variable delivery track record)

- The potential consequences of delivery problems are more severe (because the material is critical to production processes or schedules; or the organisation has low safety stocks; or because there are no alternative sources of supply or substitutes for the item concerned).

1.5   Expediting tasks may then consist of:

- Ensuring that delivery deadlines and specifications are clearly set out – and, if any changes are made, that these are clearly communicated and agreed
- Maintaining project and production schedules, and time-phased materials requirements (eg in a materials requirements planning system). A project expediter may maintain critical path network charts and/or Gantt charts showing the optimum and latest times at which supplies are required for each stage of the project. For regular supplies, a simple diary system may be sufficient to 'flag' which orders need to be expedited on a given day or week
- Monitoring or enquiring about supplier progress at key stages (without 'micro-managing'), or developing a system of 'reporting by exception' (where the supplier notifies the expediter of any stage deadlines missed or potential problems identified)
- Working with suppliers to solve any identified problems. The expediter may have to persuade a supplier to give priority to the order or buying organisation; offer help with production difficulties; offer help in sourcing any materials or information which may be holding the supplier up; and so on.
- Requiring notification of despatch of goods, and using track and trace facilities (where available) to monitor their progress in transit
- Placing pressure on failing suppliers, where required: reminding them of late delivery penalties (eg liquidated damages clauses), say, or involving senior managers in problem-solving or enforcement discussions.
- Where necessary, using contingency plans to search for alternative suppliers, existing stocks or substitute goods to meet an emergency shortage due to delivery delay.

The role of the expediter

1.6   The role of expediting will vary from company to company. The role will commence directly after the purchase order has been awarded. The aim is to ensure the timely delivery of equipment, materials and documentation in order to meet deadlines.

1.7   The role will involve both internal and external liaison. Internally the expediter will link with project managers, technical experts, finance, warehouse and logistics depending on the procurement being expedited. The expediter acts as a single point of contact for all delivery related communications. This role will increasingly involve updating computer systems, particularly in supply chain or project management systems, to ensure that stakeholders in the purchase or project are aware of the current situation.

1.8   The role requires the expediter to maintain good relationships with suppliers, often in difficult and pressurised situations. The reason why expediting begins after the order has been issued is to ensure the order is well managed through to delivery and problems and issues minimised should they occur. Expediting is carried out in two ways: desk expediting and field expediting.

1.9   **Desk expediting,** usually by telephone and email, is the most common approach and is important in monitoring order progress with manufacturers. Especially at milestones of a project, desk expediting can be helpful to check whether the project is still within the agreed schedule. Although desk expediting is a quick and easy way to be informed about the current status of a project, it should always be conducted in combination with field expediting to securely verify the actual status.

1.10 **Field expediting** means the inspection and control of the goods and materials on site. Commonly used on projects, this approach gives a comprehensive review of the exact current status of orders together with a projection of the future planning and status. Being on site can help enable the expediter to identify possible problems and bottlenecks that could lead to potential delays.

Project management

1.11 Expediting has a key role to play in large-scale projects where delays caused by late deliveries or sub-standard goods and materials can have serious effects on the timeline of the project. The expediter will play an integral role in the project, monitoring the deadlines and milestones of the project and ensuring that the supplier will deliver on time.

Supply chain management

1.12 Supply chain management involves liaison with numerous suppliers. Keeping deliveries on schedule can prove challenging. Delayed delivery of materials, products or equipment can prevent completion on time and on budget. The role of the expediter in supply chain management can involve a wide and complex area of internal and external communications, including the following aspects.

- Coordination of expediting with all suppliers
- Monitoring the dispatch of material
- Expediting visits
- Field and desk expediting
- Inspection
- Recommendations for necessary measures
- Reporting
- Situation assessment
- Supplier performance monitoring

Classifying orders

1.13 A good expediting system should prevent problems from arising as well as reacting when a late delivery occurs. However, we should be aware that not every order needs to be expedited and that some products are more important to us as a business than others. An efficient expediting system will, therefore, place our orders into different categories, perhaps like this:

- *'A' type order*. Those thought important enough for us to make a planned visit to the supplier to make sure that nothing is about to go wrong. These products are often referred to as 'strategic' because they are so important to our organisation.
- *'B' type order*. Those that require us to take action by telephone or email. Less important than 'A' orders but, nevertheless, sufficiently important for us to make sure they arrive on time.
- *'C' type order*. Those we need to progress only if our supplier does not deliver the goods by the due date. Although this action is purely reactive we need to know that nothing has gone so wrong that the goods might never arrive.
- *'D' type order*. Those we would progress only if we are specifically asked to. This might occur if a customer decides to order goods from us earlier than expected or we can foresee a need for any other reason.

1.14   If we use a simple system such as that described here, an order may not remain in its allotted category. Some orders may take on a higher priority and others may have a reduced priority.

1.15   Of course we need to make sure that, having categorised our orders, we do in fact expedite them. We can do this with a simple diary or we can set up a computerised system which prompts us by printing a list of orders we need to chase today. It is also important that we should record the results of our expediting to save us doing the same job twice.

2   Problem solving

2.1   Problems are inevitable in buyer-supplier relationships. Procurement professionals will spend a considerable amount of time solving operational, quality and delivery problems.

2.2   These processes are time-consuming and costly, and involve a number of people in both the buying and supplying companies. Such issues will often be discovered by the purchaser, but the resources needed to solve them will most likely be with the supplier.

2.3   In a perfect world no expediting would be needed but in reality there are various errors that cause shortages including: poor inventory records, quality problems, inaccurate specifications, supplier capacity problems, poor forecasting, and lost orders. Buyers must therefore be aware of the basics of expediting.

2.4   **It is not always the supplier's fault.** Some internal problems that can cause the need for expediting are poor inventory records, poor forecasting and frequent schedule change which cause problems further down the chain for suppliers. When expediting, make sure you know who caused the problem. A tough approach, when the supplier was not at fault, can make the situation worse.

2.5   **Hold regular follow-up meetings.** Even though the buyer is often not doing the day-to-day expediting, he must be advised of the poor supplier delivery performance. Having the buyer attend regularly scheduled meetings is a good method to keep people informed of actual or potential supplier problems.

2.6   By the nature of the role expediting involves confronting often difficult situations. To ensure effective problem solving the expediter needs to ensure he is well briefed and understands the problem and the issues surrounding it. There is often a need to be persistent An effective expediter gets all the details and is continually asking questions such as: Can you work overtime? How many can you make in an hour? What operation are the parts at? How many operations are left to complete? How many pieces will be done by this afternoon? How many can you ship now? What is the bill of lading number of the shipment that just went out? How can we help?

2.7   Good expediting may involve the expediter going up the supplier's chain of command until he gets an acceptable answer. If the inside sales contact or the normal contact can't get an acceptable answer then progressing further up the chain of command will often produce results.

2.8   One often overlooked area in expediting is the area that requires the most experience and creativity. The good expediter must look for other options to relieve the shortage problem. Is there an alternative part that can be substituted? Can another supplier produce the part more quickly? Are parts available from a distributor, dealer, another customer or from another division of the company? The buyer should be involved in this stage to look for other options to fulfil the requirement.

2.9   It is important to measure how suppliers are performing, especially in regard to on-time delivery. There are many ways that supplier performance can be measured. Using figures showing how suppliers are performing against other suppliers is an effective tool during scheduled meetings.

2.10   If the root cause of the error is the supplier's, the buyer should require a corrective action plan from the supplier. If the supplier doesn't improve then the buyer should investigate other alternatives.

2.11   Problem solving requires inter-personal communication between the parties. Communication is necessary to gather relevant information, and effective problem solving is highly related to the information flow.

2.12   Managers (and staff) need to be able to inform, explain and specify solutions clearly to all those involved. They need to ensure motivation from all those involved, which cannot be taken for granted. Different individuals are motivated by different forces and demands on their time. Good communication co-ordinates and explains the situation to all those involved. How the communication is facilitated affects the atmosphere and the relationship.

2.13   Within supply chains problem solving is seen as a feature of collaborative relationships together with flexibility, information exchange, and restraint in the use of power. In these types of relationships, joint problem solving between the parties is often seen as adding to the relationship success. The parties are more willing to help each other out. The closer the business relationship, the more similar the values, attitudes and goals and the higher the level of trust between the parties.

3   Tracking the relevant documentation

3.1   There are various key documents used by organisations in the procurement process. Computer systems have revolutionised document management, particularly when companies form close business relationships and integrate their systems. Many companies do not integrate to this degree and use a combination of computer-based systems supported by paper-based documentation.

3.2   When expediting an order one frequent problem area is in tracking the correct documentation. Systems and processes will be in place using computers, email and/or post but it is still a feature of modern business that paperwork tends to get lost. To understand the implications we need to be aware of the key documents and their roles in the purchase process.

Purchase order

3.3   As we saw in Chapter 3, a purchase order is a commercial document issued by a buyer to a seller indicating types, quantities, and agreed prices for products or services the seller will provide to the buyer.

Advice note (from the supplier, notifying delivery of the order)

3.4   The advice note is a document sent by a supplier to a customer to inform him that goods he ordered have been despatched. It usually gives details such as the quantity of goods and how they have been sent. Often sent electronically in advance of delivery, it notifies interested parties such as procurement and warehousing of an impending delivery. This is good practice as it allows for the onward movement of the goods to be scheduled.

Goods received note (confirming receipt of the order)

3.5   The goods received note (GRN) is generated whenever a delivery is made to a business. The GRN details what goods and quantities have been received and when. A copy will often be sent to the Finance Department so that they can match it to the purchase order. When the invoice is received, this is matched to the purchase order and GRN. Only if the details on all three match up will the invoice be paid.

Quality inspection forms (checklists)

3.6   Quality inspection is the act of monitoring or observing a process, procedure or service to ensure that all customer requirements are met.

3.7   Quality inspection checklists are designed to make sure that the expected quality of a product is as stated in the contract and that all work has been performed satisfactorily to the client's expectations.

Invoice or statement (request for payment)

3.8   An invoice is a commercial document sent by a provider of a product or service to the purchaser. The invoice establishes an obligation on the part of the purchaser to pay, creating an account receivable. An invoice typically contains the following details.

- Date
- Names and addresses of customer and supplier
- Contact names
- Description of items purchased, either products or services
- Price of goods
- Due date for payment

3.9   Invoices will track the sale of a product for inventory control, accounting and tax purposes. Many companies ship the product and expect payment on a later date, so the total amount due becomes an account payable for the buyer and an account receivable for the seller. Most invoices nowadays are transmitted electronically, rather than being paper-based. If an invoice is lost, the buyer may request a copy from the seller.

Obtaining written confirmations

3.10   It is good practice that a supplier should be expected to acknowledge a purchase order promptly.

3.11   There is often an acknowledgement slip or document attached to the purchase order, for the supplier to annotate (if necessary) and sign. This acceptance makes the contract come into being. With electronic systems the acknowledgement can be returned authorised with an electronic signature from the supplier.

3.12   In order to facilitate the supplier returning the acknowledgement many computer systems attach a separate acknowledgement form to the procurement order for the supplier to sign and return with the required details.

3.13   Acceptance of the purchase order creates a legal contract. For this reason above all others the supplier is required to complete written confirmation of the order. Although many procurement departments try to make this process as simple as possible it will often take many reminders before suppliers acknowledge the order in writing.

The role of documentation in payment

3.14   When expediting an order one potential problem area is paying the supplier. The principle used by many companies is that three documents are required to facilitate payment: the purchase order, the supplier's invoice and the goods received note.

4   Review agreements made

4.1   Organisations in both public and private sectors are facing increasing pressure to reduce costs and improve overall performance. New regulatory requirements, globalisation and increases in contract complexity have resulted in an increasing recognition of the importance and benefits of sound and effective contract management.

4.2   The increased use of computer-based systems in contract management has improved the contractual process. A more structured and formal approach to contract management has been the result. The analysis of performance indicators throughout the life of the contract provides the purchaser with an accurate and relevant negotiating tool.

4.3   Contract management is 'the process of systematically and efficiently managing contract creation, execution and analysis for maximising operational and financial performance and minimising risk'.

4.4   Successful contract management depends on thorough pre-award activities, sound administration and regular and systematic contract reviews. It is important to recognise that problems are bound to arise which could not be anticipated when the contract was raised and agreed.

Changes to contracts

4.5   Changes are almost inevitable during the life of a contract, particularly in larger and more complex construction and service contracts. Effectively managed, these can provide opportunities to improve the contract overall.

4.6   However, any changes will affect the viability of the contract for either party. If a change or modification results in a reduction in the value, the organisation could be faced with claims for increases in charges or, at worst, legal action for misrepresentation (eg in relation to the volumes stated in the contract).

4.7   Changes to the contract are easier to manage when planned. Changes will require negotiation with the supplier and the scheduled introduction of agreed changes. A change in one area will often affect other areas so any changes need to reflect all possible eventualities.

Contract administration

4.8   This activity is concerned with the practicalities of the contract, in particular the routine administrative and clerical functions.

4.9   Changes that occur during the life of the contract need to be recorded. Formal change control procedures should be designed and set out in the original contract documentation in order to avoid misunderstanding and to ensure clarity.

4.10   As part of the post-award activities of a contract these procedures should include keeping all contract documentation up to date and consistent in order that all parties have a common view. For more complex contracts where service level agreements (SLAs) are applied, a formal document management system should be established and applied, recording any agreed changes.

Contract review

4.11 Contract reviews should be carried out at regular intervals in line with the complexity of the contract. As we have seen, over the life of a contract there will often be changes and amendments. A contract review provides the opportunity to clarify these amendments with suppliers. The contract review also gives the opportunity to discuss issues of concern to both buyer and supplier.

4.12 Prior to the completion of any contract, and in time to allow the findings of the review to be implemented, it is important to undertake a review. This has the following purposes.

- To determine what action, if any, should to be taken in relation to the future delivery of the goods or services
- To determine whether the contract has met the needs of users and delivered the outputs and outcomes identified at the time the contract was initially established
- To assess the effectiveness of the contract

Contract extension or expiry

4.13 In some circumstances, it may be desirable to extend the existing contract, rather than seek new tenders or quotations for the delivery of the goods or services. A contract should only be extended where the original contract provided for an extension, ie provided for options to extend.

4.14 Contracts should only be extended with the approval of senior management and following a full review of the performance of the current supplier. As a general rule, contracts should not be extended if the market since the previous tender has changed substantially or the nature of the goods or services required has substantially changed.

4.15 If the goods or services provided under the contract are no longer required, then the contract can be allowed to expire. Despite this, some contract provisions (such as warranty, insurance and guarantee commitments) may extend beyond the life of the contract and may need to be monitored beyond the expiry date.

Chapter summary

- In a perfect world, orders would not need to be expedited. In reality, buyers must always be alert to the need for 'chasing' suppliers.
- Desk expediting and field expediting are two aspects of the task.
- To make a plan for expediting it is important to classify our orders. Only the more important ones will be expedited.
- Problems inevitably arise in the processing of orders. Buyers must be mature and professional in dealing with these.
- It is important to have good controls over the various documents involved in the procurement cycle.
- It is important to review contracts in force with suppliers. In some cases it may be appropriate to extend a contract, or to let it expire.

 ## Self-test questions

Numbers in brackets refer to the paragraphs where you can check your answers.

1   Define 'expediting'. (1.1)

2   List tasks involved in expediting. (1.5)

3   Distinguish between desk expediting and field expediting. (1.9, 1.10)

4   What options might a buyer suggest if a supplier is struggling to fulfil an order? (2.8)

5   What details are typically contained on a supplier's invoice? (3.8)

6   What activities are included in contract administration? (4.10)

CHAPTER 9

Effective Communication

Assessment criteria and indicative content

3.2 Describe the importance of effective communication with suppliers and customers to achieve timely deliveries

- The perceptual process
- Interacting with other people and building rapport
- Effective communication

Section headings

1. The communication process
2. Barriers to communication
3. Effective communication in the supply chain
4. Interaction and rapport

1 The communication process

Purposes of communication

1.1 Communication is – to use the most basic definition – the transmission or exchange of information. Our concern here is communication with supply chain stakeholders: members of the procurement team, customers, suppliers etc.

1.2 People communicate for a number of general reasons – any or all of which may be relevant to the task of supplier communication and management.

- To exchange information: giving and receiving information required in order to initiate or facilitate actions or decisions (the basis of transactions and collaboration)
- To build relationships: giving information in such a way as to acknowledge and maintain the relationship between the parties – building rapport and trust
- To persuade: giving information in such a way as to confirm or alter the attitude of another person, securing acceptance, agreement or compliance with the communicator's views or wishes.
- To confirm: giving information that clarifies and fixes previous communication, ensuring that both parties have the same understanding and aids to recollection (including evidence, if required).

1.3 In addition, parties will have a more specific purpose for communicating: an outcome that they want from a particular message or exchange of information. Knowing exactly what you want to achieve is an important element in successful communication.

The communication process

1.4 Effective communication is a two-way process, often shown as a 'cycle': Figure 9.1. Signals or messages are sent by the communicator and received by the other party, who sends back some form of confirmation that the message has been received and understood.

Figure 9.1 *The communication cycle*

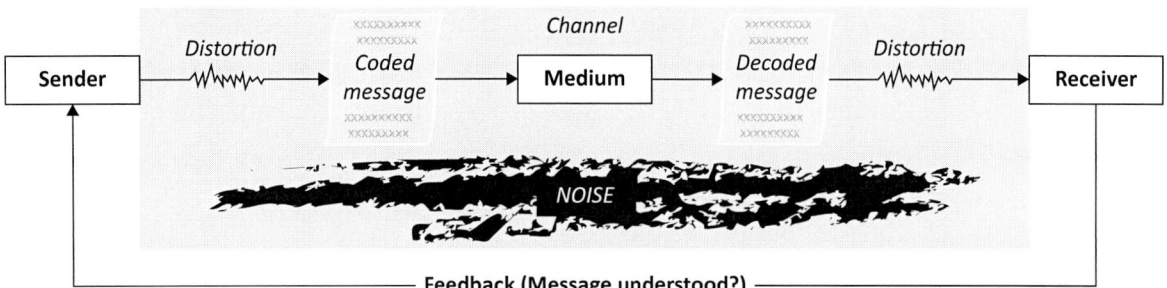

1.5 This may equally be described as a process consisting of six basic stages or steps.

- The *origination* of the message by the sender or source
- The *encoding* of the message
- The *sending* or transmission of the message
- The *decoding* of the message
- The *reception* and understanding of the message by the receiver
- *Feedback* by the receiver to the sender

1.6 The *code* or 'language' of a message may be verbal (spoken or written) or it may be non-verbal, in pictures, diagrams, numbers or body language. The needs and abilities of the target recipient should be borne in mind: not all codes will be accessible to other people. An obvious example may be dealing with overseas suppliers or customers for whom English is not their first language, but the principle would also apply to the use of technical terminology (sometimes called 'jargon') with non-specialists, or the use of unlabelled diagrams in a report.

1.7 The choice of communication *medium* (letter, memo, email, report, presentation or telephone call) and *channel* of delivery (telecom system, notice board, internet or postal system) depends on a number of factors.

- Speed: a phone call, for example, is quicker than a letter
- Complexity: a written message, for example, allows the use of diagrams, figure working, detailed explanation – and allows time for recipients to study it at their own pace
- Interactivity: face-to-face and phone discussion allows the flexible exchange of questions and answers, which is particularly effective in problem solving, negotiation and conflict resolution
- Confidentiality: private interviews or sealed letters can be limited to their intended recipients. Conversely, if swift widespread dissemination of information is required, other methods will be more appropriate: a notice board, public meeting or website, say.
- Evidence: written records are often required as confirmation of business and legal transactions
- Cost-effectiveness: for the best result at the least expense.

1.8 *Feedback* is of vital importance, since it ensures that communication is a two-way process. Feedback from the recipient to the sender allows both parties to check whether and to what extent the message has been received and understood. Feedback includes verbal messages ('I got your message. I'd just like to clarify...'; 'what do you mean by...?'), non-verbal cues (scratching the head in a perplexed manner, nodding, making encouraging noises – 'uh huh' – and so on), and action in response to the message (eg fulfilling orders or instructions accurately – or failing to do so).

1.9   It is the communicator's responsibility to adjust the message, in response to negative or doubtful feedback, until he is satisfied that it has been correctly understood. So, for example, if a purchaser wants to ensure that a supplier understands that an order is urgent, it is up to the buyer (a) to emphasise or highlight the information appropriately and (b) to check that it has been taken on board.

Written communication

1.10   Written methods are often used for formal communication in and between organisations, in formats such as letters, memoranda, reports, forms, contracts, plans, instructions and emails.

1.11   Key advantages of written communication are as follows.

- It allows perusal of the content at the user's pace, with opportunities to make notes, check facts and review the content repeatedly if necessary: this makes it particularly helpful for detailed, complex material.
- It can be shared in identical form by more than one party, and stored for as long as necessary: this makes it particularly helpful for shared plans and standing instructions – and for contracts, which can be checked and confirmed, and appealed to in any dispute about agreed terms.

1.12   The main disadvantage of written communication used to be the time required to prepare, amend, file and send hard-copy messages (using internal and external mail systems). However, word processing and email technologies have enabled written documents to be efficiently edited – and almost instantaneously stored, retrieved and transmitted to multiple recipients.

Oral communication

1.13   Oral communication follows the same communication cycle as written communication, with the important addition of immediate interaction: you switch between 'sending' (speaking) and 'receiving' (listening) constantly. There are also more signals to take into account, with the additional element of 'non-verbal' communication: tone of voice, and – in face-to-face discussion – body language.

1.14   Oral communication can be face-to-face (as in discussions, interviews, meetings and presentations) or audible only (as by telephone).

1.15   A particularly important area of professional skill development is **listening skills**. People in business spend much of their day listening, and doing so effectively can offer important benefits: listening is a quick, direct source of information – if used accurately.

1.16   Passive listening (letting information 'wash over you') is distinguished from active listening, an approach which seeks to enter into co-operative dialogue with the speaker, in order to gain maximum understanding and empathy. Active listening involves skills such as:

- Demonstrating attention: eg by leaning forward, or maintaining eye contact

9

- Giving encouraging and clarifying feedback: using verbal and non-verbal encouragers (nods, 'uh-huhs'), asking questions, summarising or paraphrasing to check your understanding
- Keeping an open mind: using your critical faculties to test the speaker's assumptions, logic and evidence – but not jumping to hasty judgements
- Being patient: waiting for a suitable opening to respond, focusing on what the speaker is saying (not on planning your own comment or response)
- Paying attention to non-verbal cues and processes: listening for underlying messages and feelings (and reflecting them back to the speaker – the technique of empathy – where appropriate).

2   Barriers to communication

The perceptual process

2.1   Communication is universal – but that doesn't mean it is easy.

2.2   Difficulties may occur because of general faults in the communication process. There may also be particular barriers in a work (or supply chain) situation because of individual differences and the complexity of organisational relationships and politics. Some of the common faults and blockages in organisational communication are shown in Table 9.1.

Table 9.1 *Barriers to communication*

FAULTS IN THE COMMUNICATION PROCESS
• Distortion or omission of information by the sender
• Misunderstanding due to lack of clarity or use of technical jargon
• Noise: a technical term for interference in the environment which prevents the message getting through clearly. It may involve technical breakdown (eg a bad phone line or loss of email connection), environmental interference (eg noise in a call centre or office, making it difficult to hear what is being said to you), or psychological interference (eg emotion or prejudice getting in the way of hearing or understanding).
• Distortion: a technical term for ways in which a message is 'lost in translation' (eg because of the use of jargon, or general misunderstanding).
• Non-verbal signs (gestures, posture, facial expressions) which contradict or undermine the verbal message, so that the sender's real meaning is in doubt
• Communication overload: the recipient is given too much information to digest in the time available
• Differences in social, ethnic or educational background, compounded by age, gender and personality differences, creating barriers to understanding (and/or cooperation) –including differences in language or accent, different assumptions and different communication styles
• Interpersonal conflict, which may reduce or prevent communication, or magnify the effect of differences
• Perceptual selectivity: people hear only what they are motivated and willing to hear
• Perceptual bias or distortion: eg stereotyping (assessing an individual on the basis of assumptions about the group to which he belongs); halo effect (forming a general impression based on single characteristics); projection (assuming others share your thoughts and feelings); and attribution (believing yourself responsible for successes, and others as responsible for failures).
• Lack of communication skills

Continues . . .

BARRIERS IN THE WORK OR SUPPLY CHAIN CONTEXT

- Lack of opportunity or respect for upward communication in an organisation (eg managers not listening to the feedback of operational staff)
- Units, functions and supply chain partners having different priorities, methods and perspectives, creating potential for misunderstanding
- Functional specialists using technical jargon which is not understood by others
- Organisational and inter-organisational politics leading to competing parties withholding, distorting and mistrusting information (especially in adversarial relationships)
- Hoarding of information, in the belief that 'knowledge is power'
- Subordinates or suppliers overloading managers with detailed information, rather than reporting by exception or summarising
- Subordinates or suppliers avoiding being the messengers of 'bad news' (especially about their own performance)
- Information which has no immediate use tending to be undervalued or overlooked
- Conflict and competition between individuals, groups or firms, reducing the willingness to communicate effectively
- Paranoia about confidentiality and competitive advantage, restricting openness in communication with partners outside the organisation

---

2.3 A more general difficulty is what Laurie Mullins (*Management and Organisational Behaviour*) refers to as the perceptual process. Mullins makes the point that 'we all see things in different ways … we all have our own, unique picture or image of how we see the 'real' world'.

2.4 Mullins gives the example of a message from senior management addressed to section heads, asking for statistics of overtime worked within their sections during the past six months and projection of overtime for the following six months.

2.5 Although each section head reads the same wording in the message, their reactions vary greatly.

- One sees it as a reasonable and welcome request to provide information which will lead to improved staffing levels.
- Another sees it as unreasonable, intended only to enable management to exercise closer control over the sections.
- Another has no objection to providing the information, but is suspicious that it may lead to possible intrusion in the running of his section.
- Another sees it as a positive initiative by management to reduce costs and improve efficiency.

Overcoming the barriers

2.6 Depending on the nature of the barrier, an organisation may try to improve its communication flows (internally and/or with its supply chain) in various ways.

- Training staff in communication skills (eg active listening, interpretation of body language, presentation of information, using audience-appropriate language, reporting by exception, giving and seeking feedback)
- Training staff in use of communication tools (eg effective use of the telephone, email, fax and so on)
- Dealing with identified 'noise' factors in the communication environment (eg maintaining communications equipment, using acoustic screens to minimise background noise, clarifying misunderstandings as they arise, or briefing staff on cultural differences likely to cause misunderstanding with overseas contacts)

- The use of 'redundancy': using back-up communications to ensure that a message gets through (eg following up a telephone conversation with an email confirmation)
- Encouraging upward and cross-functional communication by providing more and better channels (eg using suggestion schemes, employee consultation groups, quality circles, review and feedback meetings, cross-functional teams or briefings, liaison officers and so on)
- Reducing the effect of politics, conflict and fear (eg by conflict resolution mechanisms; senior management encouraging, modelling and rewarding open and honest communication; educating managers not to 'shoot the messenger' and so on)
- Protecting confidentiality where required (by contract and procedure), but also building trust as a foundation for the more open sharing of information.

2.7 If an exam question asks you about barriers to communication and how to overcome them, remember to focus on ways of overcoming each of the specific barriers you have mentioned: this is a good way of avoiding an un-contextualised, waffly answer...

2.8 As well as internal information flows, of course, it is important to manage communication with external stakeholders and contacts. This has the following effects.

- The organisation develops and maintains a network of useful contacts, which may be a source of: environmental intelligence; ideas and innovations; best practice information; influence and support; business development opportunities; new suppliers and customers; and so on
- The organisation maintains a consistent and coherent 'front' and image to the outside world (without mixed or conflicting messages being conveyed by different representatives)
- The organisation develops and maintains efficient and effective working relationships (based on information flows) with supply network partners and stakeholders.

3 Effective communication in the supply chain

Letters

3.1 A letter is a written (or printed) communication addressed to a specified person or organisation by a specified person or organisation. It obeys certain conventions of layout and format. It has traditionally been sent via the postal system, but can now be sent electronically via fax or email.

3.2 As you may see from our definition, a letter is an extremely versatile medium and format, which can be adapted to almost any purpose for writing. At the same time, its direct person-to-person nature makes it particularly well suited to private, confidential or 'sensitive' communications, and to the expression of agreements between parties.

3.3 Letters are often used in business for the following purposes.

- To express informal agreements, where a more complex legal contract is not required. You may have received such a letter confirming an offer of employment, for example. Letters of agreement are often used as a foundation for commercial contracts.
- To 'cover' (introduce, summarise or explain) more complex documents and deliveries in an accessible and personal way
- To convey information in a way that acknowledges the personal nature of the contact. Letters are often used to make and adjust complaints, to convey sensitive information (such as notification of redundancy or termination of contract), to express congratulations – and other relationship-maintaining communications.

3.4 A business letter generally incorporates certain standard elements, laid out according to the 'house style' adopted by the organisation.

Memoranda

3.5 A memorandum (or 'memo') is a standardised format which can be efficiently used to send a wide variety of messages within an organisation. Nowadays, internal email often substitutes for hard-copy memos, which used to be written or typed on standard memo pads. Memo format can be used for short reports, briefings or instructions, brief messages or 'notes' and any kind of internal communication that is more clearly conveyed in writing (rather than face-to-face or by telephone).

3.6 The versatility of the memo means that its structure and style will vary according to the nature of the message being conveyed, and the target audience. It is particularly worth bearing in mind that the audience of a memo will generally be people within your organisation or business network. This means that you may be writing to fellow specialists, and so be able to use technical language and complex ideas – but not necessarily: a memo to all staff (eg about new purchase requisition procedures) might cover a wide range of fields and abilities.

Emails

3.7 Email (or electronic mail) is a communication channel: it can be used to send a wide variety of message types (eg letters, internal memos, notes and other brief messages), with lengthier documents (such as briefs, reports or diagrams and maps) as file attachments.

3.8 Email has some major advantages for internal and external supply chain communication. It is easy to use; cost-effective (where computers and internet access are already available); versatile; fast (almost instantaneous); available for 24/7 global communication, regardless of distance, office hours and time zones; usable for one-to-one or mass communication (by sending to a recipient group); and supported by a range of helpful software tools (such as address book management, notification of receipt, the ability to attach files and hyper-links to websites and so on).

3.9 Many organisations establish guidelines for the use of email, however, because there are also some potential downsides. Email messages are easy to send off quickly (even by accident) and with the impression of anonymity, so there is a risk that offensive, misleading or ill-planned messages can damage relationships or cause misunderstandings. They also have legal effect, so firms can be sued for libellous, offensive or misleading messages. Email is not as private or secure as it seems, and may therefore be risky for confidential messages. Email can be used excessively, to the exclusion of more appropriate forms of communication. It can also be abused, where employees waste time and resources on excessive personal use of the system.

3.10 In order to use email effectively, the general principles of written communication apply: consider your audience, consider your purpose in writing, and plan the content, structure and style of your message accordingly. If you are asked to write an email in an exam, use a memo-style format: the headings are standardised for you by your email management programme (eg Microsoft Outlook). For exam purposes, invent email addresses for sender and recipient, in the format: 'name@company.com', or something similar.

3.11 Stylistically, you need to be aware of the effect of this particular medium. Bear in mind that humour and irony do not come across well in brief, typed, computer-mediated messages.

Remember to identify yourself and your subject clearly: users receive a lot of unsolicited junk email (SPAM) and you don't want your business message to be mistaken as such. Check your message carefully before you click on 'send': you can't recall a hastily sent message. Become aware of email etiquette and customs: for example, the use of capital letters is INTERPRETED AS SHOUTING. And follow any house style guidelines of your organisation (eg in regard to electronic signatures, disclaimers and other elements).

Reports

3.12   'Report' is a general term for 'telling' or 'relating', which may suggest a wide range of formats used in your organisation. You might report to your team leader with a verbal account, or write an email or memo informing someone of facts, events, actions you have taken, suggestions you wish to make and so on. However, there are also conventions to a written business report, which should be borne in mind, in addition to any house style conventions used by your organisation and department.

3.13   Routine reports are widely used for progress and performance monitoring in organisations. Examples include budgetary control reports, sales reports, project progress reports and so on. In addition, special reports may be 'commissioned' for one-off planning and decision-making. Examples include a procurement or marketing research report, a feasibility report for a proposed project, or an investigation into a particular issue.

3.14   A formal report is highly structured: split into logical sections, each referenced and headed appropriately, for clarity and ease of navigation. The recipients of reports are often managers, who do not have time to wade through confused or excessive data.

3.15   The written style of a formal report should generally be: objective and impersonal (presenting facts in a balanced way); pitched for non-specialist users where necessary; clearly laid out; concise, relevant and at an appropriate level of detail (usually placing detailed background or supporting information in separate, clearly-referenced 'appendices' at the end of the report).

3.16   Some reports may be made using standardised formats or forms. Examples include spreadsheets for cost reporting, pre-printed accident report forms, damaged goods reports or customer service and feedback reports. In such cases, the details to be provided will be clearly specified, often using tick boxes or 'delete as appropriate' options to save time and focus the content. Some sections may invite the writer to provide details: the important thing here is to be brief (although space may make this necessary in any case) and factually clear and accurate.

Preparing documentation

3.17   A wide variety of documentation may be used in the procurement cycle, and in information flows across the supply chain. Examples include purchase requisitions, purchase orders, goods inwards receipts, invoices, export and import documentation (bills of lading, customs declarations and so on), supplier appraisal or vendor rating forms – and many others, which you will encounter in your procurement studies.

3.18   The essential points (how to communicate effectively within the supply chain using available communication tools) are as follows.

- To use the available tools and standard documents where possible, since they are designed to be the most efficient, complete and (where relevant) legally valid formats for the job

- To prepare documentation according to the procedures and guidelines laid down by your organisation, in accordance with the procurement and communication procedures established
- To prepare documentation effectively, paying attention to accuracy, legibility, clarity, conciseness and other values of good communication. Consider the needs of the various users of the information, and your purpose in recording and sending it.
- To manage documentation efficiently: ensuring that copies are made, filed and sent as required by the administrative purpose of the documents; batching work on preparing documents, where possible, as a principle of good time management; and minimising wasted time and resources (eg by using electronic documentation where possible).

Communicating by telephone

3.19 The telephone is an important tool of supply chain communication. It may not be *sufficient* for all types of information exchange – since it lacks the concreteness of written communication for legal agreements and detailed information perusal – but it is particularly good for the following purposes.

- Establishing initial contacts: because it involves non-verbal communication (tone of voice etc), it is a good tool for establishing rapport
- Investigating, problem-solving and 'chasing' progress: because it is immediately interactive, you can ask questions and receive answers swiftly and flexibly
- Handling sensitive issues: the use of non-verbal cues and interactivity increase your ability to respond sensitively to the other party, eg for a complaint adjustment, conflict resolution, asking for assistance and so on
- Prior notification and subsequent confirmation of other communications or actions: the speed and cost-effectiveness of a phone call allows you to warn others to expect a letter or email, for example, and to check afterwards that they have received it
- Maintaining inter-personal contacts: 'touching base', re-establishing rapport, networking and so on.

4 Interaction and rapport

Interactions between buyers and suppliers

4.1 One key relationship driver is the **quality of interactions** between the parties. In customer relationships, this is represented by 'service encounters': the relationship depends on the supplier's ability consistently to fulfil customer expectations and to create a positive experience of doing business, at every encounter and touch point with the organisation. A single disappointing service encounter – and/or a firm's subsequent poor response to handling the problem – may be sufficient to reduce customer loyalty, or even get them to take their business elsewhere.

4.2 Similarly, in supplier relationships, each contact and transaction may represent a positive or negative episode, which will build or undermine trust, create goodwill or conflict, enhance or impede co-operation – and, over time, make each party more or less 'desirable' to do business with. Suppliers, intermediaries and potential network allies may choose not to develop an ongoing relationship with an organisation if they have a poor experience of dealing with it – especially if the potential value from the relationship is relatively small or unprofitable for them.

4.3 **Trust** is central to the success of supply chain relationships. It reduces the risk of doing business together, and supports mutual investment in the relationship. If customers distrust a supplier, for example, they are unlikely to believe advertising claims, make large purchases, share confidential information, or try new, potentially risky products or services (eg buying over the internet, or buying financial services).

4.4 **Transparency** is a willingness to share information. It depends on trust, because information can be misused: used to the advantage of one party at the other's expense (eg exploiting information on a supplier's problems to strengthen one's bargaining position); or released to unauthorised third parties (including a firm's competitors). Transparency supports a relationship by enabling a mutual understanding of both parties' needs, concerns and potential contributions: it is the basis of collaboration. Conversely, lack of transparency can cause suspicion and mistrust: consider the effect on customer relationships if information is withheld about the reasons for a product recall; or on employee relationships, if rumours of mass redundancies are not clarified…

4.5 **Commitment** is the intention or desire of one or both parties to continue in a relationship, and to invest in maintaining it. If parties are committed to the relationship, they are more likely to be loyal and reliable, and to contribute to shared goals – over and above mere compliance with contract terms or basic expectations. Commitment is therefore important for adding value and minimising risk, especially in long-term supply chain relationships.

4.6 **Co-operation** and collaboration foster relationships. One of the key principles of relationship management is that commercial relationships can be co-operative rather than adversarial or competitive: buyers and suppliers, and even competitors, can work together to add value, to mutual benefit, in supply chains and networks of alliances. Collaboration is increasingly also embracing consumers, who were previously regarded as passive recipients of marketing messages, products and services. You should be able to think of many emerging examples (especially online) of customer self-service (eg travel bookings); user-generated content (eg Wikipedia); consumer feedback surveys to improve products and services and so on.

4.7 **Mutuality**, exchange and reciprocity are all terms to express the idea that both parties gain some benefit from the relationship, and ideally share the benefits and risks of the relationship fairly between them. Mutuality is essential for any sustainable business relationship: if both parties don't get something out of it, the relationship will be exploitative (which may be seen as unethical) – and probably short lived.

Rapport

4.8 Rapport may be defined, most simply, as the sense of relationship or connection we have when we relate to another person.

4.9 We have 'positive rapport' with people we find warm, attentive and easy to talk to: we are inclined to feel comfortable and relaxed with them, or attracted to them. We all know from experience that some people are easier to relate to than others. Some individuals seem distant or uninterested in us, or we feel less comfortable around them: we would call this low or negative rapport. (Fortunately for leaders, this is not a matter of personality, but of behaviour: establishing positive rapport is a skill which can be learned.)

4.10 Rapport is a core skill for influencing, in simple terms, because: 'influencing is easier if the other person feels comfortable with you; if they feel they trust you; if they feel you understand them' (*Gillen*). In more detail, rapport:

- Helps to establish trust and a belief in the common ground between you and the other person: your viewpoint is then more likely to be received openly, rather than defensively.
- Is the basis of the positive influencing approach, sometimes called **pacing and leading**. First you 'pace' the other party (listening to, empathising with and reflecting back their views, feelings and needs). This earns trust and rapport from which you can 'lead' (influence) the other person (eg by reframing the problem or changing the emotional tone of the discussion).
- Creates a reason for people to agree with you, or do what you want them to do, because they like you. (A powerful motivator, even in business contexts...)
- Overcomes some of the barriers created by power imbalances and differences or conflicts of interest, reducing the tendency towards adversarial or defensive attitudes.

4.11 Key **rapport-building techniques** are based on the idea that it is easier to relate to someone who is (or appears to be) *like* us in some way; with whom we share some beliefs, values, interests or characteristics; and who treats us as a valued and interesting person. Some useful techniques therefore include:

- Subtly matching or 'mirroring' the other person's posture, body language and/or volume, speed and tone of voice. (This also reflects their mood and helps them to feel understood.)
- Picking up on the other person's use of technical words, colloquialisms and metaphors – and using them too (if you can do so with understanding and integrity) or incorporating them in comments and discussion summaries.
- Picking up on the other person's dominant way of experiencing and expressing things, which tend to be based on sight, sound or feeling ('I see what you mean', 'I hear what you're saying', 'That just hit me') and using similar modes of expression ('Do you see?', 'How does that sound to you?', 'What's your feeling about that?')
- Listening attentively and actively to what the other person is saying; demonstrating this with encouraging gestures, eye contact (where culturally appropriate) and so on; and asking supportive questions or summarising, in order to show that you are interested and want to understand. (This is the first-order skill of **empathy**.)
- Finding topics of common interest, and emphasising areas of agreement or common ground where possible
- Remembering and using people's names.

9

Chapter summary

- Communication is the transmission or exchange of information.
- Communication can be described by a model consisting of six basic steps: origination; encoding; sending; decoding; reception; feedback.
- Written methods of communication are more formal, but slower, than oral communication.
- There are many potential barriers to effective communication.
- Methods of communication include letters, memoranda, emails, reports, telephone and face-to-face communication.
- An important aspect of buyer-supplier relations is the quality of interactions between the participants. This depends on trust, transparency, commitment, co-operation and mutuality.
- Rapport is the sense of relationship or connection that we have when we relate to another person. It is a core skill for influencing supply partners.

 ## Self-test questions

Numbers in brackets refer to paragraphs where you can check your answers.

1   List general reasons why people communicate with each other. (1.2)

2   List six stages in the communication process. (1.5)

3   List skills involved in active listening. (1.16)

4   What is meant by the perceptual process, and what is its relevance to communication? (2.3–2.5)

5   List methods of overcoming barriers to communication. (2.6)

6   What are the particular advantages of email as a method of communication? (3.8)

7   List key elements in the quality of interactions between supply partners. (4.3–4.7)

8   List techniques involved in building rapport. (4.11)

CHAPTER 10

Forecasting

Assessment criteria and indicative content

3.3 Describe the use of forecasting to achieve timely deliveries of supplies

- The use of forecasting
- Subjective and objective techniques in forecasting
- The difficulties associated with forecasting

Section headings

1. The use of forecasting
2. Subjective techniques in forecasting
3. Objective techniques in forecasting
4. Difficulties associated with forecasting

1 The use of forecasting

Introduction

1.1 In order to manage stocks and ensure that we turn stock over efficiently, we need to consider demand, usage and lead time. Where these are fixed, as they sometimes are, there is no problem. However, they are often unpredictable. In such situations, we need to be able to **forecast** our requirements as well as the lead time of items required in order to plan stock levels and stock turnover. In this section we will consider how forecasting might be carried out.

1.2 Customer service can be addressed by forecasting what products customers will want and manufacturing or holding stock to meet the forecast. The key to having the right inventory in the warehouse is to forecast and make, or buy in, the right product. The accuracy of the demand forecast is vital but is difficult to ensure. Forecasts are effective in certain areas such as predicting stable demand, tracking sales trends, dealing with seasonality and projecting the effects of cyclical changes. They are not so effective when demand and/or supply is erratic.

1.3 Forecasting is a key element in effective inventory management. The main element in forecasting is 'prediction'; to make effective predictions of future requirements is key to the whole process.

1.4 Predictions are generally made by using the following sources of information.

- Historical usage data
- Current data and information such as that available from suppliers on usage
- What is happening within the marketplace
- Any future predictions based on supply and demand.

1.5 For example if product prices are falling demand may increase, whereas if product prices are rising demand may fall. Rising demand may lead to stockouts and supply shortage problems, whereas falling demand may lead to slow moving and obsolete stocks. Therefore all forecasts and predictions require constant revision in order to maximise their accuracy.

1.6   Forecasting is the process of estimating future quantities required, using past experience as a basis. It is fairly easy to predict the pattern of demand for some stock lines. For example, if an item is obsolete, demand will almost certainly decline as time progresses. If a special sales campaign is to be started, demand should rise. Seasonal items, such as Christmas decorations, will have a fluctuating demand. Very often, however, the position is not so obvious, and can only be found by keeping records of past performance and projecting them into the future by forecasting.

1.7   As we have already said, our estimates of future demand depend heavily on our knowledge of historical demand. We will now look at the sources from which we can obtain historical data.

Historical demand

1.8   Historical demand is past information about a company and is used to help forecast the company's future. Companies that have a progressive attitude to forecasting will gather, collect and collate data and information about their activities. This is partly because they need to report to government and other organisations in the form of tax returns and regular statistical reports but more practically because information and trends from the past can often be used as a model for the future.

1.9   Historical data is the basis of demand forecasting. Based on past historical data related to procurement and supply chain activities we can project into the future. Relevant data might include past sales levels, commodity prices over time, shipping and road haulage costs, quality and re-working issues, supplier performance, number of purchases, average value of purchases and so on. These can provide the basis for developing a statistical model that can be used to forecast future demand.

The changing face of forecasting

1.10   Forecasting has always been one component of running a business. However, forecasting traditionally was based less on concrete and comprehensive data than on face-to-face meetings and common sense. In recent years, business forecasting has developed into a much more scientific endeavour, with many theories, methods, and techniques designed for forecasting certain types of data.

1.11   The development of information technologies and the internet provided a boost to this process. Companies adopted such technologies not only into their business practices, but into forecasting schemes as well. Nowadays, projecting the optimal levels of goods to buy or products to produce involves sophisticated software and electronic networks.

1.12   Forecasting attempts to pinpoint key factors in business production and to extrapolate from given data sets to produce accurate projections for future costs, revenues, and opportunities. This normally is done with an eye toward adjusting current and near-future business practices to take maximum advantage of expectations.

2   Subjective techniques in forecasting

Classifying approaches to forecasting

2.1   Approaches to forecasting can be divided into two main categories: subjective methods and objective methods. A subjective method involves the use of subjective judgement, whereas an objective method appears to be more 'scientific'. Quantitative methods involve calculation of demand by means of numerical manipulation. At bottom, though, even apparently scientific methods of forecasting depend heavily on the judgement of the person doing the forecasting.

2.2   Subjective forecasting techniques generally employ the judgement of experts in the appropriate field to generate forecasts. A key advantage of these procedures is that they can be applied in situations where historical data are simply not available. Moreover, even when historical data are available, significant changes in environmental conditions affecting the relevant data may make the use of past data irrelevant and questionable in forecasting future values of the time series.

2.3   For example, suppose that historical data on petrol sales are available. If the government then implemented a fuel rationing program, changing the way petrol is sold, one would have to question the validity of a petrol sales forecast based on the past data. Qualitative forecasting methods offer a way to generate forecasts in such cases.

2.4   We will look at three qualitative methods in this section before moving on to quantitative methods in the following section. The three qualitative methods are expert systems, test marketing, and the Delphi method.

Expert systems

2.5   Expert systems come in two types. Firstly, at the simplest they are a grouping of experts in a particular business area (eg sales, supply chain management etc) that are brought together to discuss possible future scenarios and to predict future developments and events. This is a very focused way for companies to gain an insight into the thinking of people in a particular industry on how it might develop.

2.6   With the growth of long-term relationships between companies the concept can be extended further to allow people of similar disciplines in partner companies to meet to discuss issues.

2.7   Secondly, an expert system may be a computer based system which possesses a set of facts or knowledge about an area of human expertise. By manipulating these facts intelligently the software is able to make useful references for the user. These systems make use of rules of inference to draw conclusions or make decisions within defined areas.

2.8   Their effectiveness comes from the presence of facts and procedures which have been identified by human experts as the key components in the problem solving process. In recent years developments in computer hardware and software have facilitated the use of expert systems in industry.

2.9   Valuable knowledge can disappear with the death, resignation or retirement of an expert. Recorded in an expert system, it becomes eternal. To develop an expert system is to interview an expert and make the system aware of their knowledge. In doing so, it reflects and enhances that knowledge.

2.10 Expert systems offer many advantages for users when compared to traditional programs because they operate like a human brain. Equally they can suffer from one of the problems of the human brain – information overload.

Test marketing

2.11 Test marketing is one of the tools of market research and is often used as a forecasting technique in connection with the launch of new products. It can also be used to demonstrate how a product would sell under actual conditions by a limited or regional product launch which is based on the anticipated structure of the intended launch.

2.12 The objective is to test the entire marketing programme, in miniature, in a limited geographical area. Because the smaller test market will model what will happen when the product is launched nationally or internationally, the marketer hopes to be able to forecast the overall demand for the product with some accuracy.

The Delphi method

2.13 The 'Delphi' method in essence seeks to impose a statistical rigour and to counter the argument of bias that frequently accompanies the gathering and use of 'expert opinion'.

2.14 The term Delphi refers to the site of the most revered oracle in ancient Greece. The objective of the Delphi method is the reliable and creative development of ideas or the production of suitable information to aid decision-making.

2.15 The Delphi method involves group communication by experts who are geographically dispersed. Questionnaires are sent to the selected experts by post or email and are designed to elicit and develop individual responses to the problems posed. The responses are considered and refined with subsequent questionnaires to develop a group response.

2.16 A main consideration of the Delphi method is to overcome the disadvantages of conventional committee action where individuals may dominate, bias may develop or groups may polarise in their thinking. The group interaction in Delphi is anonymous, as comments made are not identified to their originator. A panel director or monitor, whose role is to focus the group on the stated objectives, controls the interaction between group members.

2.17 To operate successfully the participants should understand the process and aim of the exercise although there is some debate on the level of expertise required from the 'sages'. Armstrong and Welty suggest that a high degree of expertise is not necessary while Hanson and Ramani state that the respondents should be well informed in the appropriate area.

2.18 The Delphi method has proved useful in answering specific, single-dimension questions. There is less support for its use to determine more complex forecasts that involve multiple factors.

3 Objective techniques in forecasting

3.1 Quantitative forecasting uses 'hard' data, such as figures for historical demand, as a basis for statistical forecasting. Quantitative forecasting methods are used when historical data are available on variables that are of interest. These methods are based on an analysis of historical data concerning the time series (period of time) of the specific variable of interest and possibly other related time series.

Simple moving average

3.2 We begin our look at objective techniques for forecasting demand with the use of simple moving averages. As the name suggests, this is a simple technique. All we do is to look at the demand for recent periods, and assume that demand for the coming period will be the average of that experienced in the past. There is no particular rule about how many past periods we should take into account. If we are trying to estimate demand during July we might, for example, look at the actual demand experienced during January to June, and take the average of those six months.

3.3 Suppose that usage of an independent demand material was as follows in the months of January to June.

Month	Usage in litres
January	450
February	190
March	600
April	600
May	420
June	380
Total usage January to June	2,640

3.4 Using a simple moving average we would simply take the average of these six months: 2,640/6 = 440 litres. This would be our estimate of usage in July.

3.5 The reason for the term 'moving' average is that each month we move along by one step. Thus in estimating usage for August, we discard the January figure above and replace it with the figure for actual usage in July. Our estimate for August is therefore based on the six months preceding August, namely February to July.

3.6 Of course, this procedure is really a bit too simple. It is clear from the figures that demand for this material fluctuates quite markedly. The figures for January to June show a low of 190 litres, and a high of 600 litres. The simple average of such figures does not inspire confidence. The actual figure in July might turn out to be either of these extremes, in which case our estimate of 440 litres will prove wide of the mark. The next method tries to inject greater sophistication into the estimates.

Weighted average method (or moving weighted average)

3.7 The simple moving average gives equal weight to each of the figures recorded in previous periods. In the example, the figure for January contributed exactly as much to the averaging calculation as did that for June. This does not take account of a fact which is very commonly observed in practice, namely that older figures are a less reliable guide to the future than more recent figures. If there is any gradual change taking place in our pattern of usage of the item, it is more likely that the change will be reflected in our usage for June than in the figure for January six months ago.

3.8 To take account of this, the technique of moving weighted average can be used. This is designed to give greater weight to the figures experienced in recent months, and to reduce the weight given to older figures.

3.9 In our earlier example, suppose that we decide to base our estimate for July on just the four previous months (March to June inclusive). We could recognise the higher importance of recent months by giving a weighting of 0.4 to the June figure, 0.3 to May, 0.2 to April and 0.1 to March. (These weightings are not fixed – we can exercise judgement in fixing them – but they must always total to 1 if the arithmetic is to make sense.)

3.10   Our estimate for July would then be calculated as follows:

$(0.4 \times 380) + (0.3 \times 420) + (0.2 \times 600) + (0.1 \times 600) = 458$ litres

Extrapolating historical data

3.11   In the calculations above we have been using historical data and assuming that it provides a guide to the future. This process is known as extrapolating historical data to form forecasts of demand.

3.12   Like any forecasting technique, extrapolation is subject to uncertainties. This is especially the case when major changes are expected. For example, suppose we are about to launch a major advertising and promotional campaign. This may mean that demand for our products will reach levels greatly in excess of previous demand. Using extrapolation in these circumstances is less reliable, because the mathematics of the technique are based on the assumption that future demand will be roughly in line with historical demand. Where this assumption is not valid, we have less confidence in extrapolation.

Time series methods of forecasting

3.13   Another objective approach to forecasting is the use of time series. In a time series, measurements are taken at successive points or over successive periods. The measurements may be taken each day, week, month, or year, or at any other regular (or irregular) interval. While most time series data generally display some random fluctuations, the time series may still show gradual shifts to relatively higher or lower values over an extended period. The gradual shifting of the time series is often referred to by forecasters as the **trend** in the time series.

3.14   **Trend analysis** is another way of making forecasting predictions. Here, the information used to make forecasts is 'subjective' rather than the 'objective' data above. There are four basic patterns of demand.

- **Steady trend**: An increase or decline in demand is moving with a predictable pace that can easily be forecast.
- **Fluctuating trend**: The rise or fall in demand is volatile or unstable and reliable predictions are therefore difficult to achieve.
- **Rising trend**: Demand rises at a steady pace and can easily be forecast on historical data; this may have implications for material supply if demand continues to rise.
- **Falling trend**: Demand falls at a steady pace and can easily be forecast on historical data; this may have implications for stocks becoming slow moving or obsolete.

4   Difficulties associated with forecasting

4.1   Virtually every company needs to generate forecasts of their sales in the short to medium term. Being able to forecast demand more accurately has major commercial advantages.

- To plan procurement, production and inventory levels
- As the basis of marketing or sales planning
- For financial planning and reporting, or budgeting

4.2   However, within real world markets, many factors conspire to make accurate sales forecasting difficult to achieve.

4.3   Sales forecasts are frequently used for all the purposes suggested above. This leads to conflicts between optimism and pessimism and potentially introduces internal 'political' influences into the process. Examples are the different role of the profit forecast (probably conservative) and the sales plan (probably optimistic), or where marketing expenditure is loosely linked to the sales revenue of products (and therefore leads to defensive forecasting to protect planned marketing spends).

4.4   There are also conflicts in terms of which units should be forecast; orders-based for production forecasting or invoice-based for financial forecasting? Forecasts by week of the total usage of each stock item for the next 12 weeks may be required by production planning. But this time horizon is far too short and this level of product and time detail is potentially much too detailed for marketing and sales planning purposes.

4.5   The important point is to have a clear vision of who the primary customer or customers of the forecasts are. Select the appropriate level of detail and time horizon accordingly and accept that secondary customers of the forecast will probably have to accept sub-optimal forecasts.

4.6   A further difficulty associated with forecasting is the very nature of the markets. They frequently exhibit some or all of the following characteristics.

- Frequent promotional activity
- High level and variety of competitor activity
- Promotions are seldom at the same time each year
- The size of the distribution 'pipeline' tends to vary
- Growing concentration in sales to biggest customers

4.7   Future sales demand can be satisfied if we can forecast what products customers will want. We can then manufacture or hold stock to meet the forecast. The key to having the right inventory in the warehouse is to forecast and make, or buy in, the right product. The accuracy of the demand forecast is vital but is difficult to ensure. Forecasts are effective in certain areas such as predicting stable demand, tracking sales trends, dealing with seasonality and projecting the effects of cyclical changes. They are not so effective when demand and/or supply is erratic.

4.8   All these factors make it difficult for commonly used forecasting approaches such as statistical forecasting to provide acceptable results over a short to medium time horizon.

Safety stock

4.9   Safety stock is related to the accuracy of forecasting, and in fact depends on the forecast error. If the forecast error is large, the safety stock will also have to be large and if the error is small, a low safety stock is indicated. The level of service desired must also be taken into account. At a service level of 98%, there should be 98 chances in 100 that stock will be available when called for. It might be impracticable to aim for 100% service, but the higher the service level the more safety stock will be needed.

4.10   Simple forecasting techniques are not usually suitable for the control of raw materials and bought-out parts for manufacturing organisations or construction companies, where demand is strictly related to a pre-planned operational programme. Even in these firms, however, it may usefully be applied to general consumable stores.

4.11   In situations where demand is independent (ie demand for one item bears no relationship to the demand for other items), decisions as to how much to stock will be based on the inventory manager's view of the probabilities of different levels of demand arising. These probabilities will, to some extent, be subjective, ie some measure of opinion or judgement will be employed in their determination.

Forecast deviation

4.12   It is fairly easy to predict the pattern of demand for some stock lines. For example, if an item is obsolete, demand will almost certainly decline as time progresses. If a special sales campaign is to be started, demand should rise. Seasonal items will have a fluctuating demand. Very often, however, the position is not so obvious, and can only be found by keeping records of past performance and projecting them into the future by forecasting.

4.13   However sophisticated the system of forecasting may be, it will not be 100 per cent accurate and there will be a difference between forecast and actual usage. This is known as **forecast error** or **forecast deviation**, and allowance must be made for it. In a perfect situation where the forecast was 100 per cent correct every time, and where the supplier always delivered promptly, the pattern of stock would be in perfect flowing lines of supply and demand.

4.14   Accuracy of forecasts is, therefore, variable. A manufacturer's annual production plan would be expected to be more accurate than a hotel's forecast of annual guest numbers, for example. Forecasting is particularly important in the retail sector where a forecast, not only of annual sales of an item but also seasonal variations would be required. Many companies use sophisticated computer packages to carry out this kind of forecasting. Inventory, of course, is purchased based on the forecast and held until it is required.

4.15   A trend may emerge due to one or more long-term factors, such as changes in population size, changes in the demographic characteristics of population, and changes in tastes and preferences of consumers. Forecasters often describe an increasing trend by an upward sloping straight line and a decreasing trend by a downward sloping straight line. Using a straight line to represent a trend, however, is a simplification because in many situations nonlinear trends may more accurately represent the true trend over time.

4.16   A number of factors might therefore influence forecasts, depending on the nature of the market, and the systems used by the organisation.

- Objective data: historical usage patterns and data (eg from internal operational records) and data supplied by other stakeholders (eg distributors' or customers' EPOS systems)
- Subjective data: eg market research and opinion-based analysis of trends and environmental factors

- Seasonal or cyclical variations in demand (eg due to seasonal buying, the seasonality of the product, business cycles – boom and recession – and so on)
- Trends (or specific changes) in consumer demographics and behaviour, technology development, market prices, competitor activity and other environmental factors affecting demand

4.17 A number of factors will also impact on the *accuracy* of demand forecasting.

- The availability of past demand and usage data from which to extrapolate trends
- The validity and reliability of research and forecasting methodologies
- The skill and objectivity of forecasters
- The degree of change and unpredictability in the market and wider environment
- The accuracy of available information, and the quality of information sharing and communication with suppliers and customers

Chapter summary

- Forecasting is an important technique in the effective management of stocks.
- Key sources of data for forecasting include historical usage data, current data from suppliers, developments in the marketplace, and future predictions of supply and demand.
- Techniques used in forecasting may be either subjective or objective. However, even apparently scientific and objective methods rely greatly on judgement.
- Subjective techniques include expert systems, test marketing and the Delphi method.
- Objective techniques include simple moving average, weighted moving average, and time series methods.
- There are many difficulties associated with forecasting, which means that there will always be a forecast error or deviation.
- A large forecast error or deviation implies a need for high levels of buffer stock.

Self-test questions

Numbers in brackets refer to paragraphs where you can check your answers.

1   List possible sources of information used in forecasting. (1.4)

2   Distinguish between subjective and objective techniques for forecasting. (2.1)

3   What is an expert system? (2.5, 2.7)

4   How does the Delphi method work? (2.15)

5   How does a simple moving average work? (3.2–3.6)

6   Describe the additional refinement in the use of a weighted moving average. (3.7)

7   List market factors that make forecasting difficult. (4.6)

Subject Index